THE
TECHNIQUES OF MODERN
HITTING

THE
TECHNIQUES OF MODERN
HITTING

Wade Boggs
David Brisson

A Perigee Book

Perigee Books
are published by
The Putnam Publishing Group
200 Madison Avenue
New York, NY 10016

Unless otherwise noted, all photos copyright © 1990 by Donn Bruns.

Wade Boggs is represented by Coordinated Sports Management Group, Inc., 790 Frontage Road, Northfield, IL 60093.

Library of Congress Cataloging-in-Publication Data

Boggs, Wade.
The techniques of modern hitting / Wade Boggs and David Brisson.
p. cm.
ISBN 0-399-51595-X
1. Batting (Baseball) I. Brisson, David. II. Title.
GV869.B6   1990   89-28471 CIP
796.357′26—dc20

Printed in the United States of America
1 2 3 4 5 6 7 8 9 10

This book is printed on acid-free paper.
∞

Contents

Prologue
Listen to Me: Be You

I don't want you to hit like Wade Boggs. What's right for me may not be right for you. I *do* want to help you help yourself at the plate, and that's what this book is about.

Did you know in the minor leagues we didn't even have a hitting coach? If you were stuck in a slump, you solved it on your own or it stuck. The manager was too busy filling out lineup cards, tossing batting practice, handling pitchers, and making sure players made curfew. That's why a hitting book like this can really help, and—thanks to my dad—I'm living proof.

My dad's the best student of baseball I know. He was a great fast-pitch softball pitcher, and who knows more about hitters than pitchers? Dad taught me that the best way to make contact is to wait for the ball, and he always had a tip when my swing was off—which is why he gave me a hitting book in the first place.

It happened my senior year at Plant High School in Tampa, Florida. Pitchers were pitching around me, and I was walking a lot. I didn't think

that was fair, and I felt frustrated and started swinging at bad pitches. Soon, I began grounding and flying out and found myself in a terrible rut. Then, Dad gave me a copy of Ted Williams's book, *The Science of Hitting.*

Ted's book was inspirational. It reinforced what Dad had always said about patience at the plate, and I got myself back on track. The second half of that season I managed twenty-six hits in thirty-two at-bats. A few weeks later, I was drafted by the Red Sox in the seventh round, I signed my first pro baseball contract, and I began a six-year journey to the big leagues.

To be honest, I never thought I'd write a book about hitting until after my career was over. But the more I talked to young hitters, the more young hitters I wanted to reach. I've learned a lot from teachers like Ted Williams, Charlie Lau, and Walt Hriniak; but baseball has changed, and I've developed some new theories to prepare you for today's pitching and make you a better hitter.

You may not want to apply all the tips and techniques you're going to

I never thought I'd write a book about hitting until after my career. But baseball is changing fast, and I felt now was the time to tell you what I know.

learn—that's up to you. Your best bet is to take what works and leave what doesn't. So don't rush as you read. Think about it. Study the photos, review the text, test out what you learn, and have *fun.* Baseball is challenging and builds character, but it's also a game to be enjoyed. Above all: Listen to me, but be you.

NEVER GIVE UP

I'm living proof that dreams *can* come true. Ever since Dad and I listened to Curt Gowdy call the baseball game of the week on Saturday afternoons in the sixties and seventies, my ambition in life was to become a major leaguer, play in an All-Star Game, and win a World Series.

I've attained the first two of these goals and came one pitch away from the third playing against the Mets in the 1986 World Series. Even so, I was never an instant or automatic success. In fact, I spent most of my minor-league career platooning with other players, and I watched a lot more games from the bench than I'd like to remember.

The reason is that third base is a power-hitting position, and the Red Sox wanted me to hit fifteen or twenty home runs a season. I was hitting six to eight each year in the minors. So even though my average was between .300 and .340, there always seemed to be another third baseman ahead of me on the depth chart. Often, I'd have to fill in at second, short, and first base to get in any playing time at all.

Even after I led the International League with a .335 average and had

167 hits and 41 doubles in 1981, the Red Sox brought nine of my teammates to the majors in September (when active rosters expand to forty men)—but left me behind. Let me tell you—that hurt. I began to wonder if I'd ever get my shot.

Finally, the next winter, the Sox named me to the forty-man roster, and I began the 1982 season in Boston pinch-hitting and backing up Carney Lansford at third. Lansford was a proven hitter, one of the league's best. In 1981, he led the majors with a .336 average, and in the field he ate up everything hit near the bag. Nobody was going to replace Carney, let alone a rookie. So I watched, learned, made the most of my playing time, and hoped that someday I'd get my chance.

Unfortunately, it came when Carney broke his ankle in late June that year, but I made the most of it. For the next six weeks, as Carney mended, I replaced him at third and went on a tear that made it nearly impossible for the Red Sox to sit me down. When Lansford came back, I became the starting first baseman and wound up setting the rookie record for batting averages. I hit .349 in 338 at-bats—just 100 plate appearances shy of qualifying for the American League batting title.

The next year the Red Sox traded Carney, and I became the starting third baseman. I also won my first batting title, and I've been secure in my job ever since. My point is: Dreams *can* come true. So, never give up on yourself. Don't quit the team just because you're not playing as much as you like. Work at it. If you want something badly enough, you'll

This sign at Plant High School always sends me the same important message: Dreams can come true.

find more often than not that you can get it as long as you keep striving.

Your role may seem set in concrete, but baseball is subject to change. So, if you're not playing, work twice as hard to improve your game. Don't quit. When you're on a team, you're just as much a part of that team as the guy who bats .300 or hits forty home runs. You may only get one hit in a season, but it might be the one that wins your league championship or state title. So, whatever your dreams, go after them 100 percent. As long as you keep trying, you're never out of the game.

THE
TECHNIQUES OF MODERN
HITTING

1

An Introduction to Conscious Hitting

The only thing in sports tougher than hitting a baseball may be explaining how to hit one. In eight big-league seasons, I've talked to dozens of major leaguers who swing a bat 250 to 300 days a year—yet only a handful fully understand and can describe the keys to successful hitting.

You can't blame them. Hitting a baseball involves as many moving parts as a speeding race car, and the process happens just as fast. Every movement from head to toe must be exact on every pitch. Hitters must gear their swing up or down in a flash to keep their bat on track, and like race-car drivers, no two hitters perform 100 percent alike.

Long-ball hitters like Jose Canseco don't swing the same way as gap hitters like Kirby Puckett or technicians like Don Mattingly and George Brett. Yet, all are effective. Each can win a game with a swing, each hits for a high average, and each is pitched to with respect and fear.

The fact is, hitting is a self-styled art which is largely intuitive and unconscious. That doesn't mean hitting can't be taught: any player with knowledge and practice can improve. It means that hitting should be and feel natural—and that's what separates the great hitters from the pack.

The Cansecos, Pucketts, Mattinglys, and Bretts never force anything at the plate. Each swings freely, comfortably, and enjoyably. To these greats hitting is fun, and they approach it that way in practice and especially in games.

I feel the same way. I've loved hitting ever since I crushed a cork ball with a broomstick when I was six. And you love hitting, too—that's why you're reading my book. The fact is, the more enthused and relaxed you feel at bat, the more productive a hitter you're going to be. It all comes down to something I call Conscious Hitting: the confidence of being sure and in command at the plate.

Conscious Hitters are challenged and excited at the plate. They know

Conscious Hitters feel sure and in command at the plate. They know when, what, and how to hit. You can, too.

which pitch to swing at, when to shift their weight, and how to produce the hit each hitting situation demands. Unlike self-conscious hitters whose minds race out of control from pitch to pitch, Conscious Hitters slow the hitting process down because they know it inside out and enjoy a calm and soothing sense of control. They know where to hold their hands, how to grip the bat, and when to start and finish their swing.

Conscious Hitters believe they're better than any pitcher on every pitch and have fewer and shorter slumps because they've learned to check the hitting checkpoints that keep their swing on track.

In the pages ahead, I'm going to introduce some new hitting theories and techniques—such as the Pendulum Effect and the Power Curve—that will make you a Conscious Hitter. You don't have to be Canseco, Puckett, Mattingly, or Brett to learn to work the strike zone, recognize each pitch, and hit to all fields. All you need is knowledge and practice. Maybe your average won't shoot up fifty points overnight, but if you work at it, you'll make great strides as a hitter.

THE PERFECT HITTER

No one will ever be a perfect hitter, but I think it's important to strive for perfection every time you're up. You may get only three hits in every ten tries, but don't take that thought

You may not get a hit every time up, but you should always strive for a perfect swing on every pitch.

with you to the plate. Instead, believe you're going to get a hit every time you step in the batter's box and try to execute 100 percent correctly.

Whether you succeed or not doesn't matter; in the end, your positive frame of mind will produce more hits—and that's the point. Perfection is *the* standard for which every athlete should strive and the yardstick by which we're measured. Perfection motivates and challenges, and should always be positive. You can use perfection to stretch your abilities and raise your level of play. You should never use it to fault yourself or your teammates for making mistakes—that's how you learn.

My dad is an artist—not a Picasso or Rembrandt, but he takes immense pride in his paintings. If he sees a tiny flaw in a bird in one of his seascapes, he'll whiteout the entire canvas and start over. Even if he's put six months into the work, he doesn't get angry or upset. He knows that if he keeps at it, he'll capture his vision on the canvas and that's what he wants from his work.

My purpose is to master each hitting situation every time I'm at the plate, and I approach each at-bat with that expectation. I don't set goals, I set standards. Rather than target myself to 200 hits a season and become content if I reach that goal, I use it to assess my performance and fuel more success.

The last thing any hitter ought to do is put a cap on his productivity. Each year, I set out to hit at least one point higher, drive in one more run, and belt one more home run than the previous season. I go after the batting title every year, and I keep trying until the last swing is swung.

Always strive to be better. *Expect* to do well on every at-bat and let your good feeling ignite you to do your best. We're all endowed with different natural abilities, but who's to say how far your abilities can take you? The fact is: You never know how good you can become, so why limit yourself. Rod Carew didn't.

Rod was one of the greatest hitters in the history of baseball. He owns seven American League batting titles, averaged .328 in nineteen seasons, and was the best bunter I've ever seen. When I played against him, Rod would beat out a bunt to third in one at-bat, then line the ball by me the next time when I moved in to take the bunt away. The man was a magician. At his best in 1977, Rod knocked in 100 runs, scored 128, and hit .388.

He was one of the few hitters able to change his stance and set up in the batter's box and still crush the ball. And yet, as Rod would be the first to admit, he wasn't born with great natural gifts. He was a skinny, sickly kid from a poor family in Panama. Often, he barely had enough to eat, and his first baseball glove was a paper bag. What Rod did have, however, was a love of and devotion to hitting. He practiced on dusty sandlots day after day and was always striving to better himself at the plate. Rod never had an inkling how far his hitting would take him, but his direction was perfection every step of the way.

What other jobs can you fail at seven of ten times and still be successful?

THE PUZZLE EFFECT

Is hitting a baseball *really* the toughest task in sports? A fisherman who spends twelve hours from dusk to dawn without a nibble or a mountain climber who attempts to scale Mt. Everest might have legitimate cause to disagree. But, why argue? All I can say is, I've seen many perfect swings produce outs; you can be absolutely flawless at the plate and still fail 70 percent of the time. That might not make hitting the most formidable feat in sports, but it sure makes it tough.

What other jobs can you fail at seven of ten times and still be considered successful? You wouldn't hire a lawyer who won three of every ten court cases. And you wouldn't pass a student who got 30 percent of the questions right on a test. The fact that a .300 average is a benchmark for batting success is really a tribute to just how difficult hitting is. Trust me, hitting a white sphere 3 inches in diameter traveling at 90 miles an hour with only a stick of wood in your hands is far from easy. Even Little League pitchers can zing the ball at 40 or 50 mph, and they're only 45 feet away. And often a pitcher's speed is less than half the problem.

Today, big-league pitchers can hurl that 3-inch sphere with pinpoint accuracy using any number of pitches. Off-speed fork balls tumble toward the strike zone at the very last instant. Change-ups that look like fastballs drop to the plate with a microsecond's warning; sliders take sharp and sudden bends away from hitters; sinkers nose-dive to the knees with astonishing velocity. And no one ever knows what a knuckleball is going to do.

Today, big-league batters can face four to five pitchers in a single game—each with the ability to move the ball in a completely different way. An ineffective starting pitcher can be sent to the showers in the first inning, and every team has a corps of multifaceted relievers. If an off-speed specialist like Mike Boddicker of the Red Sox is forced out early, hitters will see a steady diet of fork balls and sliders from long and middle relievers like Dennis Lamp or Mike Smithson.

Toward the late innings, when Boston wants to force hitters to ground out, we'll go to a setup man like the now-retired Bob Stanley, whose sinkers and sidearm delivery present a different look and rhythm. Then, if we're up against a lefty hitter like Mattingly or Brett, we might bring in Rob Murphy for some left-handed heat. And, of course, there's our closer, Lee Smith, whose 95-mph fastball and curve are tough on hitters on either side of the plate.

It's no wonder there are fewer .300 hitters every year. In the National League, you're lucky to find half a dozen a season. The American League—even with designated hitters batting for pitchers—yields only an additional ten to twelve. With hitting lagging behind pitching, major-league teams are turning to batting coaches in increasing numbers. Hitting is being talked about and analyzed like never before, and there's a new emphasis on style and technique.

Today, the pitcher's edge is trickling down to every level of baseball,

The pitcher's edge is trickling down to every level of baseball. Even Little Leaguers must develop good hitting habits to compete.

and even Little Leaguers must develop good hitting habits to compete. Rate it where you like on the scale of athletic difficulty, but hitting only gets harder and more complex as you climb the ladder. The feet, legs, hips, shoulders, head, arms, and hands must all work in perfect harmony to hit effectively; and if just one body part goes out of sync, the entire process can collapse. Even a slight dip of your back shoulder or an untimely turn of the hips can derail your swing, and the need to adjust and readjust is constant for every batter.

This not only makes it hard to excel at hitting, it also makes hitting difficult to teach. Why? Because so much is happening so quickly; and each person's hitting rhythm differs according to size, quickness, and strength. I hold my bat more vertically than Dwight Evans. Dwight Evans starts with more weight on his back foot than Jody Reed. Mike Greenwell's hands finish higher than Marty Barrett's.

Every batter's hitting puzzle is put together from the same body parts, but each hitter uses them in his own way. Picasso and Rembrandt were great painters, but Picasso's brush strokes were jagged and choppy and Rembrandt's were long and smooth. Like the artist, you need to find the strokes to put *your* hitting puzzle together.

Hitting involves the same parts of the body for everyone, but each hitter must find an individual way to put those parts together in a smooth, accurate swing.

FIVE RULES TO HIT BY

Assembling the pieces of the hitting puzzle is a lot like building a house. Your stance is your foundation. Your bat and helmet are your equipment; your body is your workforce; your swing is your power source; and your hitting style is your design. And yet, whether you hit for power, average, or both, there are some ground rules of good hitting that always apply.

Naturally, you need to have your eyes on the ball and a proper swing, but I'm not referring to physical rules.

I'm talking about the strategic rules that lie at the core of Conscious Hitting. Put the simple rules to use and I guarantee you'll raise your average, hit more home runs, and do a lot more to help your team.

Once you're in the batter's box, priority number one is to *know your mission*. Most of the time that's simple: Pick out a good pitch and get a hit. But with runners on base, your mission may vary. Your job may be to hit and run or to advance a runner, get the ball up in the air to score a man from third or sacrifice bunt.

Many times the third-base coach or manager will give you a sign, and it's simply a matter of executing what you've been told. Still, the more you study each situation and ask yourself how you can best help the team, the better hitter you'll be.

A good pitcher may try to keep the ball away from your favorite hitting location, and defenses may shift to stop you from hitting to a certain area of the field. But you should always *make good contact,* and—except for sacrifice situations—your goal is always to *minimize outs.*

Good contact is your best chance to start or sustain a rally and produce a run; and it's the first obligation of every swing. Good contact minimizes outs, which is really what winning hit-

Good contact is the key to minimizing outs.

ting is all about. Too many times, I've seen rallies collapse because a hitter couldn't put the bat on the ball and ended up walking back to the dugout with the bat on his shoulder.

Striking out's no crime; everybody does it once in a while. Power hitters like Reggie Jackson accept it as part of their game. But let's face it: The only time striking out ever helps the team is when the catcher drops the ball, the runners advance, and the batter takes first base. The most strikeouts I've had in my career is 61 in 1985; that was also the year I had a career high 650 at-bats and a league-leading 240 hits and a .368 batting title—up from .325 the previous year.

One reason I hit better in 1985 was because I perfected my ability to *recognize each pitch.* (I'll explain the simple physics of it in a later chapter.) Recognizing the pitch takes away the pitcher's element of surprise and dulls his edge. Once you know what's coming, it's a lot easier to know where the ball's going—whether it will be a strike or not and whether it's a hittable pitch. Even if you're a Little Leaguer facing mostly fast-ballers, you still need to know where the ball's heading and its rate of speed. The quicker you recognize the pitch, the better your bat control and the more often you'll *swing at strikes.*

Swinging at strikes puts you in the driver's seat, and I've made my living at it. Swinging at strikes lets the pitcher know you know the strike zone and forces him to throw you bet-

ter pitches to hit. Conversely, the moment a pitcher knows you chase pitches outside the strike zone, the more he can afford to throw bad pitches and the harder it's going to be to get a hit. To minimize outs, you may want to lay off *nasty*—virtually unhittable—strikes if you have fewer than two strikes on you. The one thing you should never do is chase pitches *outside* the strike zone. Make the pitcher pitch. Don't do his work for him.

You may, on occasion, see Kirby Puckett or Dave Winfield hit a low, outside slider or a high, inside fastball for an extra-base hit—and I admire their aggressiveness. But these are two of the best big-league hitters I know. So, unless you have that kind of talent, be disciplined—swing at strikes.

THE MENTAL GAME

Ted Williams once said hitting is "fifty percent from the neck up," and he was right. You can leave the rules of good hitting in the dugout unless you have a good mental game to match. So many times, I've seen young hitters fold in the middle of an at-bat. They strike or ground out on a perfectly hittable pitch—and it's not for lack of talent. The problem is, their head game wasn't intact, and it can happen to anyone.

My year of rookie ball in Elmira, New York, is a good example of what poor concentration can mean. I was eighteen years old, away from Tampa for the first time, and very homesick.

Ted Williams once said hitting is 50 percent from the neck up, and he was right. Face each at-bat with a belief that you can do the job. Erase every doubt.

Always be aggressive and in control at the plate.

I didn't feel like myself off the field or at the plate and hit just .263 in fifty-seven games—almost 100 points below my major-league average.

Now, no matter what's going on off the field, I wrap myself in a *cocoon* state of concentration whenever I'm at the plate. When I'm in the hitting cocoon, my every thought and feeling is 100 percent focused on hitting. I'm relaxed yet aggressive, completely absorbed in my hitting rhythm, and I feel great. You may want to think of it as mental toughness or tunnel vision, but it's key to succeeding at the plate.

Another key to a good mental game is *controlled aggression.* No matter who's on the mound or how you're hitting, you're in a battle and ought to be primed to attack at all times. This is not to suggest that you forgo the ground rules of good hitting or good judgment.

The idea is to be ready to pounce on every pitch, yet be able to wait calmly for a good pitch to hit. There's nothing a pitcher likes less than an aggressive hitter in control of his emotions and his bat. Controlled aggression enables you to start your swing early enough to hit the fastest fastball and slow your swing down to hit the trickiest breaking ball. Conscious Hitters must always be aggressive and in control. Without that, no hitter's mental game can be intact.

2

Where I Stand with the Grand Masters: What Williams and Lau Really Said

Baseball has gurus and great thinkers like any other profession, and I doubt I'd be where I am today were it not for the two grand masters of hitting: Ted Williams and Charlie Lau.

In eighteen seasons with Boston, Ted averaged .344, cracked 521 home runs, and knocked in 1,839 runs. He's the only player to lead the majors in walks for six years in a row. He's the last man to hit .400, and he once reached first base in a record sixteen straight at-bats.

Ted's swing was smoother than silk, and no one had a quicker bat. Teams used to shift six men to the right of second base, pitch him low and away, and he'd still pull the ball for a hit or a home run. Ted never went for a pitcher's pitch and always swung at strikes. He was the best.

Charlie Lau proved you don't have to be a great hitter to be a great teacher of hitting. Charlie was a journeyman catcher who played on five teams in eleven big-league seasons. Charlie stroked only 16 career home runs and 298 hits; and his .321 on-base percentage is 23 points lower than Ted's lifetime batting average. But Charlie understood the hitting game and became a great batting coach for the A's, Orioles, Royals, and Yankees before he died in 1984. Charlie made Reggie Jackson a more complete hitter in Reggie's later years and helped prolong the career of White Sox catcher Carlton Fisk.

While Ted taught the basic principles and practices that made him and players of his day great, Charlie dissected photos and videotapes of hundreds of swings and introduced ideas like striding with a closed front toe and maintaining a balanced rhythmic stance to transfer weight from

Ted Williams's biggest gift to hitting was his discovery of the Impact Zone.
Courtesy of The Boston Red Sox

front to back before the ball leaves the pitcher's hand.

WHAT TED SAID

Even before my dad gave me *The Science of Hitting* my senior year at Plant, he taught me two of Ted Williams's most important ideas. The first is Weight and Wait: that is, keep your *weight* back and *wait* as long as possible on each pitch so that you don't get fooled. The second is to swing slightly up and drive the ball in the air. The slightly-up swing puts the hitter's bat on the same plane as the pitch, which comes on a downward flight from the pitcher's release point above the 18-inch-high mound.

Ted's emphasis on patience and discipline helped me learn the strike zone and to hit within its bounds. Ted also made me aware that there are hitters' pitches and pitchers' pitches. The odds of getting a hit on strikes crossing the inner and outer edges of the plate—though they vary for each hitter—are a lot less than on pitches down the middle—which is why I don't swing at every strike. But Ted's biggest gift to hitting was his discovery of the Impact Zone.

The Impact Zone is the hitting area up, down, and across the front and rear of the plate where a batter can make contact with a pitch. Ted introduced the Impact Zone to explain the geometric advantages of the slightly-up swing, but it teaches a lot more than that. The Impact Zone is really a road map that hitters can use to place the ball to any field. Batted balls hit in the front of the Impact Zone are usually pull shots; balls hit in the middle of the zone travel up the middle or to the gaps; and balls hit in the rear of the zone head to the opposite field.

Ted liked to make contact in the front of the Impact Zone and pull the ball—which is why he advised swinging with hips ahead of hands. If every hitter had Ted's quick bat, I'd say do it, too, because you'll hit a lot more home runs. The trouble is, nine of ten dead-pull hitters yank their front shoulder off the ball and *can't* pull the outside strike for a hit. And frankly, there's also an issue of time.

When Ted played, pitchers relied mostly on fastballs and curves, and the slider was just a pup. Guessing was a lot less risky, hitters had a better idea what was coming and where it would cross the plate, and a guy like Ted could get his bat in front of the Impact Zone quickly enough to pull the outside strike for a hit.

Today, however, pitchers have almost as many pitches as I have chicken dishes, and they're cooking up new ones all the time. My teammate, Mike Boddicker, for instance, throws a *fache:* a three-fingered change-up curveball that looks like a change then drops to the plate like a curve. And don't forget the bullpen. Pitchers today stay in games only as long as they're effective, and you can face four or five a game. One guy may have a burning fastball, another may have a great curve, a fork ball, a screwball, a knuckle-curve—you name it.

Look at the Oakland A's: If hard-throwing starters like Dave Stewart or Bob Welch have an off day, they'll follow with nasty sliders from Matt Young, bring in setup men like Gene

The Impact Zone stretches across the front and rear of the plate, almost to the front and back lines of the batter's box.
Contact in the rear of the Impact Zone usually produces hits to the opposite field.

Contact in the middle of the Impact Zone usually produces hits to the middle or outfield gaps.

Contact in the front of the Impact Zone usually produces pull hits.

MIKE BODDICKER

Today's pitchers are cooking up as many pitches as I have chicken dishes. My teammate Mike Boddicker invented a change-up curve he calls the *fache*.   *Courtesy of The Boston Red Sox*

Nelson or Rick Honeycutt, then finish you with the closing finesse of Dennis Eckersley.

That's why *proper waiting* today means more than making sure you don't get fooled. It means utilizing the full measure of the Impact Zone, letting the ball get in on you, and learning to hit at various locations as it crosses the plate.

A perfect example is the sinker away. That pitch comes at hitters, tails to the knees at the last second, and comes from any direction. If you swing hips ahead of hands and open your front shoulder before contact, the best you can do is hit a ground ball to shortstop. But if you wait a little longer and open your hips on contact as the ball crosses the middle of the plate, you can drive it on a line the opposite way. The same goes for the fork ball. It looks like a fastball until the bottom falls out just before the ball reaches the plate; and if you don't let it get in on you, the only thing you're going to hit is air. But if you let it get in on you, you can pluck it out of the air and shoot it up the middle for a hit.

Of course, good pull hitters hit home runs, but few hit for a high batting average and too many strike out. Even Ted Williams might have hit better if fielders had played him straight away instead of shifting way over to the right—if he had utilized the whole field as taught by Charlie Lau.

CHARLIE'S LAW

Charlie has taken a beating by the press for messing up good hitters, but that's way off base, and I want to set the record straight. George Brett's swing is textbook Charlie Lau, and he can hit through you, around you, or over you at any time. He's also one of the best clutch hitters in the game.

Charlie believed consistent hitting meant using all fields; that a hit the opposite way is just as valuable as a pull hit, and that using the entire ball park keeps the defense honest. Charlie never said you could hit a ball as far to the opposite field as when you pulled it, but you *could* hit home runs. Anybody who's ever seen Jim Rice or Jose Canseco launch one to right field can tell you Charlie was right. Opposite-field home runs might not make you take out your tape measure, but you can still take your trot.

Charlie didn't accept the slightly-up swing as Ted and I do because he thought hitters couldn't pull it off— that they'd dip their shoulders, open their hips too soon, and uppercut the ball high into the air or pop out. Instead, he believed hitters should move their hands down to the ball, level their swing through the Impact Zone, and then finish up in the shape of a V.

There's no doubt Charlie knew his stuff; but when you think about it, his swing actually *does* finish slightly up. The only difference is that Charlie said to hit on *top* of the ball; that it was safer to swing down and hit the ball low or hard on the ground than to swing up and hit it in the air. Well, that's too defensive for me, and I can't agree.

Besides, if you swing slightly down on an object coming at you from a slightly down direction you decrease your Impact Zone—which is already small enough. So, in my

book, if you want to make good contact, hit the ball just below its center and get it in the air on a *line* to the outfield. Out there, you've got three defenders compared with five on the diamond, and each has a lot more ground to cover; that's where you want to send the sphere.

Naturally, anyone who's ever heard of Charlie Lau knows that Charlie gave birth to the idea of letting go with the top hand; and yet most people haven't a clue as to what he meant. Did you know that Roberto Clemente let go? All Roberto did was hit .317, knock in 1,305 runs, and wind up in Cooperstown after eighteen seasons with the Pirates. I don't know if Roberto ever talked about letting go or even knew that he did it; nevertheless, he was one of the few who let go naturally and is clear-cut proof that it can work.

Most people think you let go on contact. The truth is, you let go just *after* contact to get maximum power to the ball and full extension *through* the ball as you finish your swing. Did you know that the two-handed finish decreases bat speed by 10 miles per hour? The reason is that your top hand has to stretch beyond its limit for you to complete your swing and automatically decelerates your swing to keep your arm from coming out of the socket.

If you let your top hand go after contact, however, your body is free to follow its natural course without slowing down your finish. The added punch might drive a hard ground ball through the hole or a long fly ball into the stands. You'll also stop your top hand from rolling over too soon and dominating your swing; and you'll have fewer topspin shots caused by making contact a shade sooner than you want.

The trouble with letting go with the top hand is simple: It's such a new concept that only a few players have been taught to do it. I've let go in batting practice every day for years. I've also tried it in spring-training games in 1987 and 1989; but subconsciously something tells me to finish with two hands during the season—that's how I've always hit, and it works. If you're just starting, the one-handed finish may be easier to learn. If not, stick with what feels best. As the saying goes, if it ain't broke, don't fix it.

Letting go just after contact increases your bat speed, but it's still new to many players and should be tried and tested before you apply it in games.

The strike zone stretches from your armpits to the middle of your knees.

3

Working the Strike Zone: Your Signature at the Plate

The strike zone stretches from your armpits to the middle of your knees, spanning the full 17 inches across home plate—some seven balls wide. If you drew a picture, the strike zone would look like a three-dimensional box packed with baseballs. Some of these balls would stack up in hitting areas that would make your mouth water. Others, you wouldn't want to swing at with an oar. Although the width of the strike zone never varies, the precise area differs for every hitter depending upon your height and setup position in the batter's box.

I stand in the middle of the box, I'm six-foot-one, and my zone is ten balls high. You may be five-foot-four and stand in the front of the box or six-foot-three and stand in back. Your zone could be twelve balls high or six balls high. And yet, no matter what it is, your job's still the same: You need to learn, work, and protect your strike zone as if it were your personal signature at the plate.

In an ideal world, that signature would be monitored electronically on every pitch. Home-plate umpires would wear beepers in their ears and a signal would go off each time the ball crossed the plate for a strike. Every hitter would have *his* exact strike zone each time up. Hitters would know the precise area to protect, pitchers would know the exact area in which to throw strikes, umpires would make correct calls on every pitch. There would be no debates, no bad calls, and no complaints.

Naturally, in the real world no such system exists. Each umpire has a different interpretation. Some shrink the strike zone, others make it big—sometimes too big. You've got low-ball umps and high-ball umps, inside-corner umps and outside-corner umps. That's why you should always pay attention to the home-plate umpire's calls—especially when you have two strikes.

Don't ever let the ump take you out of your hitting cocoon. Too many times I've seen big leaguers jaw with an ump after a called strike, lose con-

centration, and then swing at a bad pitch or strike out. So, respect the ump's calls and learn from them. Remember: Your opponent is 60 feet, 6 inches away, not 3 feet behind you.

The real key to mastering the strike zone is depth perception. Each hitter has to anticipate where and when each pitch is going and whether it's going to be a strike. Whether it's on or off the corner, too low or too high. If you like what's coming, *bang*—attack; but if a pitch is outside the strike zone or is a nasty strike— and you have fewer than two strikes—let it go.

Naturally, depth perception depends upon your ability to see the ball, and good eyesight is a big help. But you don't need 20–15 vision to know your strike zone. I know many big-league hitters with average eyesight who can tell if a pitch is 5 inches above the plate or 3 inches off the inside or outside corner. The reason is, they take a lot of batting practice during which they only swing at strikes.

Recognizing pitches gives hitters a big edge in reading distances and depths during games. Conscious Hitters also make a point of replaying every at-bat. They review which pitches they swung at, which they let go, and which were balls and strikes. This not only enhances hitters' knowledge of the strike zone, it also shows them their strong and weak hitting areas, reveals the strategy of the opposing pitcher, and familiarizes them with a pitcher's full menu of pitches.

WHEN TO BEND THE RULES

The strike zone is also a road map to hitting success, and you should swing within its borders in all hitting situations but three: the squeeze bunt, the hit-and-run, and a man on third with less than two outs.

In each case, your mission is to advance or protect the runner. When your coach calls for the squeeze, you've got to bunt the ball down or foul it to protect the runner moving from third base. When the hit-and-run's on, your job is to hit a sharp ground ball through the infield to advance the runner moving from first to second or second to third.

In both situations, contact is a must—and you may have to venture out of the strike zone. Sometimes the catcher will read the play and call a pitchout that you just can't reach with the bat. But on each play, runners are relying on you to get the bat on the ball, and you've got to jump on the pitch no matter where it is.

The only other time when you might venture outside the strike zone is with a man on third and less than two outs. I call this my "money" situation because I'm confident I can produce the RBI. But it still takes guts, and you should only go for a waist-to-chest-high pitch tailor-made to hit a fly ball to the outfield.

Other than these exceptions, the strike zone should be a signature you respect at all times and your guide to good swinging. Remember, swing at strikes during batting practice, al-

Always be ready to attack every pitch, and if it's a strike you like, go after it.

This letter-high fastball is a borderline pitch I would swing at only in a hit-and-run situation or when I'm looking to hit a sacrifice fly.

ways get a good pitch to hit in games, replay each at-bat, and stay in your hitting cocoon.

WALKS MAKE RUNS

Walks aren't a sign of weak hitting—they're a sign of smart hitting and team hitting. I don't care who says what. Walks minimize outs, set up or sustain rallies, and walks win games. A walk may not always be as good as a hit, but walks create base runners and base runners score runs. Any time you transform a two-for-five day into a two-for-four with a walk, you've

given your team one less out and one more base runner—and that could be the difference in the game.

Over the years baseball critics have charged that Wade Boggs looks for walks. Horsefeathers. Wade Boggs doesn't look for walks. Wade Boggs looks for good pitches to hit, and it's because he walks that he gets so many hits. If I don't get a good pitch and I'm seeing pitches outside the strike zone, I'm not going to help the pitcher by swinging, and neither should you. And it has nothing to do with wanting to win a batting title—it's pure common sense.

The fact is: Walks tire pitchers'

arms and send them the all-important message that you only *swing at strikes.* It's as basic a principle of Conscious Hitting as casting is to catching fish. So, don't be embarrassed by walks. Use them as part of your strategy and as a message to the opposing pitcher that you're going to work him, frustrate him, and let him make the mistakes.

If you're a free swinger like Kirby Puckett who hits .350 and fares better by letting it all hang out, don't change a thing. Go after any pitch you feel you can hit, because you're going to help the team. But if you're not—and few of us are—don't play into the pitcher's hand. A ''free pass'' is always better than a ''Do Not Enter,'' especially when your return trip to the dugout goes by way of home plate.

TAKE THE FIRST PITCH

Taking the first pitch will alert you to a pitcher's stuff and is especially good strategy against one you've never faced or on your first at-bat of the game. True, you've seen what the pitcher throws in warm-ups, but you don't know what his pitches look like from the plate. So take a pitch, put it in the feed bank, and get familiar with him. I've seen many first-ball, fastball hitters come up with nobody on or out, ground out on the first pitch, come up the next time with bases loaded, and get fooled because they didn't take the time to study the pitcher.

Don't be afraid to get behind in the count. The pitcher still has to put the ball across that 17-inch dish three times to get you out. Even if you're having trouble making contact, the rule still applies. It's better to wait for a pitch you can drive for a hit than to guess fastball on the first pitch and make an out. So, use your full at-bat, study each pitch, and get a good pitch to hit.

TWO STRIKES MEAN NOTHING

All pitchers have one thing in common. They need three strikes to get you out. So, never give up when you're down two in the count. The fact is, when you have two strikes, you've seen at least two pitches and you've got at least one more coming—and one pitch is all you need.

Besides, you might get a better pitch with two strikes than you got with one strike or no strikes. Remember, the more pitches you see, the more familiar each pitch becomes, the easier it is to hit, and the more likely it is that the pitcher is going to make a mistake. So, don't panic. Choke up a half inch if you're trying to get better bat control, and prepare to swing at any pitch near the strike zone. The two-strike count is not the end of the line. Don't let it be for you.

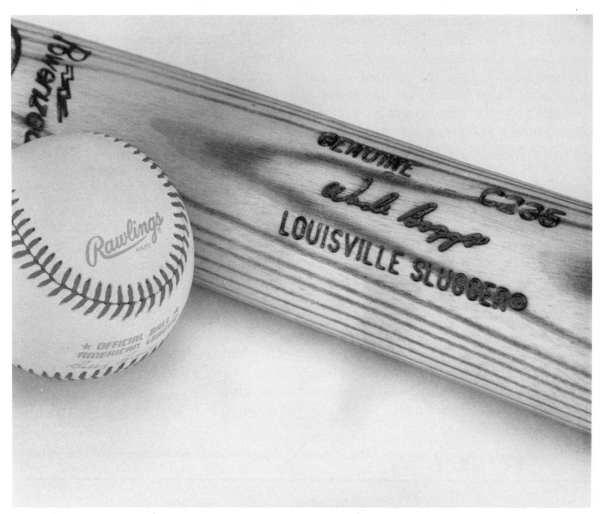

The C-235 is light enough for me to get around on a 100-mph fastball and heavy enough to keep me from bringing my bat through the strike zone too soon. It's got a large hitting surface, and it's just the right weight for me to whip my bat to the ball.

4
Preparing to Hit

CHOOSING YOUR WEAPON

Bat speed means everything to a hitter. The quicker you can swing your bat, the more often you'll make solid contact—so long as you're under control. That's why choosing a bat requires a trip to the bat rack and some testing until you find the one that's right. You're searching for a weapon light enough to get around on the pitch yet weighty enough to keep you from getting too far in front. But don't think heavy lumber leads to heavy hitting. Only a proper swing can do that.

Once you make your choice, if the bat loses its magic, don't be afraid to change. If you're young and still growing, you may want to switch to a heavier bat to add to your strength and power. Big leaguers tend to go to lighter bats to pick up extra bat speed as the season wears on and they tire; so don't balk at one that's light, either.

I'll never forget my first special bat. I found it in a dumpster when I was thirteen. I used it for two full seasons and liked it so much I nailed it together when it cracked. The reason I liked it so much was because it felt good—and that's *the* key to your se-

lection. If a bat feels right, there's a good chance it is right. It's that simple.

One thing all hitters using wood bats should look for, however, is a hard hitting surface. The harder the surface, the more punch you'll get on contact and the more likely it is that the bat's going to last. Most big leaguers believe bats with wide grains across the barrel have the densest wood. Find one with only five or six grains and they call it a pearl because it's so rare. The way I see it, any bat that's flame treated and feels good is good enough for me. To keep the barrel clean, just rub a little alcohol on the barrel and that should do it.

Personally, I like a big barrel 34½ inches long, weighing 32 ounces, and a medium-to-small handle I can get my hands around. The large hitting surface gives me more bat to put on the ball without slowing down my swing. It's light enough so I can get around on Nolan Ryan's fastball and heavy enough to stop me from lunging at Frank Viola's change-up.

But everyone's different: Don Mattingly uses the same weight bat as I do, but with a smaller barrel. My bat's too light for Jim Rice, who wants more weight. Henry Aaron used a 31-ounce bat, and so does Jack Clark. Babe Ruth used a 56-ounce bat. Tony Gwynn uses a 29-ounce bat. So, it's really a matter of what you like to swing.

The same rule applies to the aluminum bats you find in high school and college, but don't be fooled by the power they add to your swing. Aluminum is much denser than wood, and the ball jumps off the bat, traveling faster and farther on impact. I remember one player I played with during his first year in the minors. He wasn't a big guy, but he hit twenty home runs his senior year in college and fancied himself a power hitter. When he hit only three homers in Single A, he couldn't believe it—but I could. He'd been deceived by his old aluminum bat.

One final thought: Sometimes wood chafes. Don't worry about it. Turn the bat on the other side to make contact and stay with it as long as it's intact. Remember, every bat sees its final day. If it breaks or you have to say good-bye, just remember those sweet swings you took with it and smile.

GRIP: THE STRENGTH POSITION

Once you've got your weapon, you want to get a good, firm grip. If you're a big leaguer, your hands have to be strong enough to withstand the impact of a 95-mph pitch. But even Little Leaguers need the safe, snug feeling of having the bat firmly in hand. I apply a little pine tar or rosin within 18 inches of the bat handle—baseball's legal limit. A few players tape their bats or rub skin adhesives on their hands; however, the key to a good grip is making your bat one with your hands as if it were part of your body.

Holding the bat too tightly expels energy that takes away from your power at the point of contact. Holding it too loosely creates a floppy swing that can misdirect your bat or create a vibration effect on contact that reduces your hitting punch.

While there's no set way to hold your bat, there is one basic guideline: Make sure you're comfortable. Julio Franco, the hard-hitting second baseman with the Texas Rangers, grips his bat with the bottom two fingers of his bottom hand over the knob.

My grip starts as if I'm holding an ax, preparing to chop down a tree. The knuckles on my hands line up in between one another and the pinky finger of my bottom hand wraps around the knob of my bat—that's my preference. Then, as I bring the bat into the hitting position I stiffen my hold around the handle.

The same process applies to you. Once you start your swing, your grip will naturally tighten at contact. So, don't strangle or dangle the bat as you set up to swing. Make your grip strong but tension free so you can sweep your bat to the ball with maximum authority.

PROTECT YOUR HANDS

Hitting has the same effect on your hands that playing the guitar or cello has on your fingers. It'll eat 'em up if you're not careful and give you blisters if you don't pace yourself at the

Your grip tightens naturally as you swing.

Gloves protect your hands and can give you a better grip.

gloves, but they sure can swing the bat.

CHOKE UP FOR BAT CONTROL

If you need better bat control, especially with two strikes, choke up. A lot of young players believe choking up isn't manly or is a sign of weak hitting. Nonsense. Choking up is a smart move that shortens and lightens the bat. Choking up makes it easier for you to guide your bat to the ball. It will help you get around quicker against fastball pitching and cuts down loops in your swing that take your bat off target.

Ty Cobb and Pete Rose had more hits than any big leaguers who ever played the game, and they were no-

beginning of the season. For that reason, I swing just 30 minutes at a time my first month of off-season batting practice every December. After that, I've got enough calluses to hit for an hour and a half—when I really begin to sharpen my swing. Calluses stop the bat from tearing your hands up and are a big help whether you play a 22-game Little League schedule or 162 games in the "show."

Another way to improve your grip is with a batting glove. Batting gloves protect your hands and create friction to give you a better handle. Franklins work well for me, but there are several brands you can buy. And if you're not comfortable with any of these, you're in good company. George Brett and Keith Hernandez don't wear

Choke up for better bat control.

Ty Cobb, a great hitter who choked up on the bat all the time. *(National Baseball Library, Cooperstown, New York)*

torious for choking up. Lesser-known Felix Millan, who played second base for the Atlanta Braves and the New York Mets, was also a great choke-up hitter. Felix was small and trim. He didn't have the power of Rose or Cobb or the talent; but he was smart enough to use whatever resources he could to get his hits, so he always choked up.

In twelve years, Felix scattered line drives all over the field and hit a lifetime .279. It's true, Felix had very few home runs, but he once cracked thirty-seven doubles in a season and could really sting the ball. The fact is, if you hit the ball hard and high enough, you're going to get distance. There's no doubt, you can still choke up and power the ball out of the park. I've done it, and you can too.

STEPPING UP TO BAT

Once you choose your bat, you've got to be ready to use it *before* you enter the batter's box. Some hitters think about their next at-bat while on defense, causing them to lose concentration and make errors. Always avoid that. Instead, prepare to hit while you're still in the dugout. Study the pitcher, watch your teammates at the plate, and picture yourself making perfect contact before you physically step in the batter's box. Use your imagination and adrenaline to get those good thoughts flowing.

When there are still two batters ahead of you, walk over to the helmets and pick yours up. As you put it on, make it a thinking cap. Now, you're tuning in, preparing for your hitting situation, and getting ready to

bunt, advance the runner, or swing for a hit.

As you walk toward the on-deck circle, intensify your concentration. If you're a Little Leaguer or in high school, don't get distracted by the crowd or family and friends. Keep your eyes on the pitcher. Study his repertoire of pitches and how his balls move. Maybe he's tipping off his curve ball or having trouble getting his fastball over the plate.

Once you're inside the circle, stretch out. Take some practice swings. Grab a metal doughnut or another bat to loosen your muscles. If you use rosin or pine tar, put it on your bat. Keep your eye on the imaginary ball as you take your practice cuts and time your swings to the incoming pitch.

Continue to size up the pitcher. Check out his sequence of pitches and how his ball's moving, especially if you've never faced him or if it's your first at-bat of the game. Anticipate what you're going to see and continue to visualize what you're going to do when you see it. Remember this final thought: The pitcher can only attack in two ways—by working the inside and outside corners of the plate or by changing speeds up and down your strike zone.

Above all: Think good thoughts. Feel good about yourself as a hitter, and *relax*. A brand-new experience awaits you.

THE CONFIDENT HITTER

Once you get in the batter's box, always think you're *going* to do the job. *Might* never comes into it. Don't

Your preparation for every at-bat begins in the dugout a few batters before you're up. Study the pitcher, think good thoughts, and get yourself ready mentally to swing the bat.

Your helmet's like a thinking cap. The second you put it on, you're entering your hitting cocoon, gearing up to hit.

Once you reach the on-deck circle, loosen up, but make time to take a closer look at what the pitcher's got.

worry about getting hit by the pitch or making an out. Be completely positive and totally absorbed in the hitting cocoon. You're about to go into battle, and you've got to believe you're going to win. Don't look at the pitcher's face or think about him. His appearance and attitude are of no consequence to you. Your focus is 100 percent on the white sphere and the little imaginary square box above the pitcher's shoulder where he releases the ball.

Now, you're ready to assess the situation and your job. Is the defense playing you honestly? Where's the hole to drive the ball through? What does the defense tell you about where the pitcher wants to throw the ball? Still nervous? Take a deep breath.

A coach might send in a signal to let you know what to do, but most often you're on your own. So, have an idea of what you want to do. If there's a man on third with less than two outs, try to drive the ball to the outfield. If there's a man on second with less than two outs, try to hit to the right side to advance him to third. In that situation, a base hit to right will almost certainly drive in the runner.

Be selective, but stay aggressive all the time. Be ready to hit every pitch, but if it's a ball take it. Don't wait for a strike to start your swing—this will usually make you late. Instead, start your swing back early, at the peak of the pitcher's windup, and use your long glide path to control your impact zone. The more bat control you exert in this crucial area of contact, the less control a pitcher has over you.

Be selective, but stay aggressive all the time.

Stand in the middle of the box with your feet shoulder-width apart.

5

The Stance: Your Foundation at the Plate

SETTING UP IN THE BATTER'S BOX

Most hitters sense the plate under their chin and use it as a compass to set themselves in the batter's box. I set up with my feet at shoulder width apart so I'm completely balanced. My front foot is even with the plate, roughly 15 inches off the inside corner in the middle of the box. George Brett stands back in the box to buy extra time, but I like to stand in the middle.

In the middle, sinkers, sliders, and curves break right in front of you, and you have ample time to catch up to a fastball. You can also easily extend the end of the bat 1 inch over the outside corner. This gives you complete coverage of the plate, leaving out any areas of the strike zone your bat can't reach.

Once you've found the right spot, stick with it because that's your strike zone. Moving around in the box will only change your relationship to each pitch and confuse you. Curveballs will cross the plate on a different plane, sliders will break in an unfamiliar hitting area, and the pitcher will gain a decided, unnecessary advantage.

Rod Carew was one of the few big-league batters able to change his stance from pitcher to pitcher. But Rod always kept his back foot locked in the same place, so his strike zone never changed.

Another thing to avoid is crowding the plate. Crowding has a severe impact on a batter's ability to hit the inside-corner strike. If you're concerned about getting the sweet part of the bat across the heart of the plate, don't worry. That happens naturally as you extend your arms when you set up 12 to 15 inches off the plate. Crowding won't help extend your arms any faster, and you'll lose as much as one-third of your coverage of the plate.

OPEN, CLOSED, AND SQUARE

Your stance is the power base from

From where you set up in the batter's box, you should always be able to extend your bat 1 inch over the outside corner of the plate.

which you launch your swing. It's almost like the starting block sprinters use in a 60- or 100-yard dash. Your stance must give you anchorage to support your body and the spring to ignite it. It must be balanced so that you can cover the entire plate and rhythmic so that you can shift your weight back, then forward, to generate full force to the ball.

Once you set your feet, the first step is to bend forward at the waist. Next, bend your knees so that you are in a slight crouch, with your weight distributed evenly on the balls of your feet. Be careful not to squat like a catcher, because you'll jerk your bat and change planes in the middle of your swing. The more streamlined

your takeoff, the more effective your swing's going to be.

There are three basic stances you can use: open, closed, and square. Each style has special strengths and drawbacks, and no two players apply them exactly alike. The key, as always, is to choose the one that feels best and adapt it so that you're completely balanced and relaxed.

The open stance protects hitters against inside pitches and is usually the choice of pull hitters who make contact in front of the plate. To set up in an open stance, point your front foot 45 percent toward your pull side of the field. This gears you to open your hips sooner and adds to your power on pitches over the middle and

Balance is key to every stance. Your stance must give you anchorage to support your body and the spring to ignite it toward the ball.

The open stance gives you excellent coverage on pitches from the middle to the inside corner of the plate.

The closed stance gives you excellent coverage on pitches from the middle to the outside corner of the plate.

The square stance gives you balanced coverage of the plate and is the best starting point for attacking the strike zone.

inside part of the plate. The trouble with the open stance comes on pitches from the middle to the outside part of the plate. On these pitches, even a straight-ahead stride will take you away from the pitch and you'll be hard-pressed to hit the ball solidly.

The closed stance protects you against pitches away, maximizing your coverage of the middle to the outside part of the plate. To set up in a closed stance, cross your front leg slightly over your back leg so that your front foot is pointed 2 to 3 inches toward your opposite field. The closed stance sets you so that a straight-ahead stride is toward the outer region of the plate and can help a hitter whose natural tendency is to pull hips, head, or hands out too early. The trouble with the closed stance is its lack of coverage of middle-in pitches. Players with closed stances find it very difficult to pull the ball.

The square or parallel stance provides the best of both worlds, maximizing a hitter's coverage of the strike zone.

To set up in the square stance, line up your front and back feet so that they're shoulder-width apart and parallel. The square stance adds to your hitting range and flexibility. You can hit any pitch to any field because your starting position is balanced 100 percent to the middle of the field. You're not primed to hit an inside or outside pitch or to lean to any particular side. You have equal access to any part of the plate when you stride, and the likelihood of pulling your body out too early or swinging late is less.

I'm essentially square in my stance, but my front foot is slightly closed. This gives me maximum coverage of the outside corner of the plate, and I can still pull the inside pitch. The strangest stance I've ever seen belongs to John Wockenfuss, who played for Detroit and Philadelphia. John used to line up his front and back feet piggyback style with only one or two inches in between. Although it worked for him, I wouldn't recommend it to you. Your best bet is to test out as many stances as you like until you discover the one that works best. Remember, power starts from the ground up, so make your stance a good one.

UPPER-BODY POSITIONING

If the stance begins with your lower body, it ends with your upper body. Your hands, arms, head, and shoulders all play a vital role in your swing. Each should start in a position that allows you to bring your bat to the ball quickly and fluidly, allowing you to take a direct, error-free path to the ball.

THE HANDS AND THE BAT

The hands are vital to precision hitting and always seem to be young hitters' biggest problem. Some hitters like to hold them low at the waist. Others try to imitate Carl Yastrzemski and clench them high around the ear. The fact is, neither is a good position to start. Try hitting a sinker starting with your hands up around your neck or a high fastball with them low

Hold your hands at or just below your chest, 6 to 8 inches from your body.

around your hips and you'll see what I mean.

Holding your hands at the waist will cause you to jerk the bat up to get it through the strike zone. Holding the bat above your chest will cause you drop your hands down. In each case, you're wasting motion, creating a large, loopy swing, and increasing your margin of error on every swing.

You'll find it difficult to get around on sliders and fastballs, and you'll have little time to adjust to a breaking ball when you've been fooled. In my book, the best place to hold your hands is just below the chest, roughly 6 to 8 inches off your body. From this area, you can power your bat into any region of the strike zone on a straight, clear path with no wasted motion.

Here's an exercise that can help:

Set yourself in the batter's box. Pivot your body toward the mound so that your legs are side by side. Drop your bat across the heart of the strike zone and extend your arms. Then, bring your hands back to the V-position and pivot back to your stance. Wherever your hands are at this point is the starting position that you want to assume at the plate.

Once you know where to hold your hands, the next step is to decide the angle at which to hold the bat. This is really a matter of choice and comfort. Charlie Lau used to tell hitters to hold the bat at a 45-degree angle. He thought a flat bat was easier to control en route to the Impact Zone. Ted Williams preferred holding the bat in a perpendicular position because he thought it was easier to maneuver—and I agree.

Holding the bat in an upward, vertical position relieves tension in your hands and adds to your power. You won't feel a tug on your wrists as you do when you hold it flat. The weight of the bat is balanced on its center, and the bat feels lighter and easier to control. You can swing more freely and quickly. As the pitcher winds up, you may want to wiggle your hands slightly to cock them as you prepare to swing. However, if you can cock your hands better and start more quickly holding the bat flat, do it. You're the best judge when it comes to holding your bat.

The rest of your upper body should be tension free and relaxed. The last thing you want is to hold yourself so tightly that your legs are rigid or shaking. The better way is to be limber, loose, and flexible. Your top and bottom elbows should bend

Yaz was one of the few hitters with enough bat speed to hold his hands at his ears and still get his bat around on the fastball. But, unless you can hit like Carl, I wouldn't advise it. *Courtesy of The Boston Red Sox*

Holding the bat in a vertical position adds to your bat speed and power.

Tuck your front shoulder and keep it closed until the ball arrives.

in a V and be parallel to the plate. Your shoulders are always parallel to each other, but they line up differently according to your stance.

If you have an open stance, your shoulders are slightly open toward your pull side of the field. If you have a closed stance, your front shoulder points toward the opposite field with your back shoulder in a parallel position. And if you have a square stance, both shoulders are on line with the pitcher, splitting the middle of center field. The most important aspect of positioning your front shoulder is to tuck and keep it closed so that it doesn't leave the strike zone before the ball arrives.

6

The Pendulum Effect: The Never-Changing Swing

THE SWING NEVER CHANGES

No matter where you want to hit the ball or what kind of pitch is thrown at you, the mechanics of the slightly-up swing never vary.

Naturally, if you swing up to hit a low pitch, you'll hammer the ball into the ground or miss; and if you swing down at a high pitch, you'll have equally bad luck. The point is, slightly up is neither the preferred point of contact nor strictly up. Slightly up is the U-shaped pendulumlike path your bat takes from the start to finish of your swing, in and out of the Impact Zone.

The swing itself should be loose, free, and natural: not too hard and never lazy. The bottom half of your body applies the force of your weight through the ball and is your major supply of power. Your hips coil as the pitcher delivers the ball and open just after contact to clear your backside through the ball like a backhand stroke in tennis.

The top half of your body directs the bat. Your front arm is a pull-lever that drags your wood from the back to the top of your swing. Your top hand is your guide hand and should be slightly below the bottom hand on contact to generate maximum force. Your wrists are pulleys that roll naturally after contact—no need to force them to turn over. And your arms fully extend high above your shoulders as you finish.

Your head remains fixed in a proper hitting position facing the pitcher until contact, when it tilts slightly down. Your eyes are like a sonar system, zeroing in on the pitcher's release, recognizing each pitch, and following the ball.

SHIFTING WEIGHT AND SLIGHTLY UP

As I've said, your swing is a pendulum that rocks back, then forward, so that you can apply the full force of your body to hit the ball. And you can't just start from scratch. A prize-

Keep your eye on the bat barrel as you study this swing. Notice how it goes back and comes forward, then up through the strike zone to a high finish. This U-shaped, slightly-up swing elevates your bat to the same plane as the downward flight of the ball and maximizes your utilization of the Impact Zone. It's the perfect swing to drive the ball hard and far into the air.

fighter has to start back to throw a punch, a woodsman has to start back to swing an ax, and a fisherman has to start back to cast a rod and lure.

Hitters start back using something I call a trigger mechanism. The trigger mechanism transfers an additional 25 percent of your weight to your back foot as the pitcher rotates his hips in his windup so that 75 percent of your weight is back. As this transfer takes place, your front shoulder and hips close and coil and your hands fully extend back to a launch position.

As the pitcher starts to throw, everything uncoils in sequence like a windup toy. Your back leg transfers your weight back to 50–50, your front foot lands, then you make that microsecond decision to swing. Once you commit, your hands come forward, 100 percent of your weight shifts to your rigid front leg, and your shoul-

ders and hips open on contact to generate full force to the ball.

The slightly-up swing starts from the chest—or wherever you hold your hands—travels down through the Impact Zone, and finishes high above your head. It's not like a machine gun on a turret that never changes planes. Your hands don't start from your chest and finish chest high. That would be level. They don't start by your shoulders and finish at your knees, either: that's swinging down.

Slightly up looks just like the letter U and would be just like a golf swing if baseballs didn't change planes in flight. The bat begins in a vertical position above your back shoulder, levels out in the heart of the Impact Zone, and finishes high above your front shoulder.

Opponents of the upswing claim it's an uppercut that causes hitters to pop up or fly out. What they're for-

getting is that every pitch comes from a mound above to a plate below. All the upswing does is place the bat and ball on the same plane at contact, which, in effect, levels out the swing.

The fact is, the slightly-up swing is the most effective way to drive the ball in the air. Slightly up enables hitters to spend a longer period of time in the Impact Zone—where contact is made—and avoiding the uppercut is simple. The idea is to keep your shoulders parallel to the plate while the ball's in flight. Your front shoulder should remain low and closed until contact. Your back shoulder should remain parallel to the ground at all times. Once your shoulders leave the path of the ball, your body leaves with them and your swing is in the danger zone. Be careful not to dip either shoulder, or you'll pop up or hit a chopper and prove the critics right. The key is to position your top hand slightly below the bottom hand on

contact. That creates the upward arc of the bat to the ball. Once you get it right, you'll find there's no better way to hit a baseball.

Now that you've got an idea of how the slightly-up swing works, let's take a closer look at the steps involved in the process.

TRIGGER MECHANISM

The trigger mechanism is the cocking motion that gets your weight going back as the pitcher's winding up. Mine is my right leg. Yours could be your hips, hands, or shoulders. To ignite it, simply focus your energy on your trigger and shift your weight through your hips to your back leg. Try not to jerk back or lean. The movement should be smooth and natural, so be easy and stay loose.

The trigger mechanism starts your swing early, so you can wait

The swing begins as you shift your weight from front to back with the trigger mechanism. This cocking movement takes place as the pitcher winds up and must be smooth and natural.

longer on the breaking pitch yet still be primed to hit a fastball. A slow start causes hitters to commit too early, transfer their weight too soon, and spend too little time in the Impact Zone.

Once your trigger mechanism is complete, 75 percent of your weight is on your back foot and you're ready to launch your swing.

LAUNCH POSITION

The launch position is the climax of your weight shift from front to back and occurs as the pitcher releases the ball. Your hands and arms are at peak extension backward. Your front foot begins to stride forward. Your back leg is slightly bent, and your hips and shoulders remain parallel to the plate and closed.

For one millisecond, your swing actually stands still while you stop to recognize the pitch. You're prepared to swing, but you're still uncommitted. That decision comes in the last millisecond after your front foot lands and you know if you like the pitch.

LANDING POSITION

The landing position is your last step before you actually swing the bat. It starts as your front foot lands on a closed front toe perpendicular to the pitch. The landing should be as soft as walking on eggshells, and the closed front toe keeps your hips and shoulders from unloading on the ball too soon. Landing with your front foot open will open your hips too soon, causing you to lose power before

contact and veer your bat off the ball.

Once you're in the landing position, the 25 percent of your weight you triggered back goes forward and you're balanced evenly: 50 percent back, 50 percent front. Now, you're ready to shift another 25 percent to your front side and commit to swing.

CONTACT POSITION

Contact itself is like an exploding stick of dynamite. The more of the ball you hit, the more powerful the burst. You don't have too swing hard to hit far. Power comes from the bottom up when 100 percent of your weight transfers through the ball. But no one ever really sees the ball hit the bat. You always blink. It's a protective, reflexive action your eyes can't avoid, and most hitters aren't aware that it happens. So, don't think about it, just keep your eyes on the ball.

The process to contact begins just after you land. As you ride your weight from back to front, your back leg continues to bend, your front leg stiffens, and your hands begin to sweep the bat to the Impact Zone. Though your power comes from your back leg, the front leg's the one you hit off. Your hips and shoulders must move directly to the pitch, but neither opens fully until just after contact. As your bat hits the ball, your back foot lifts ½ to 1 inch off the ground, indicating you've transferred 100 percent of your weight to the ball.

The swing itself is a whipping motion—aggressive but controlled. A quick bat is critical, but reckless bat speed pulls the shoulders and hips off course, creating a wild, inaccurate

The launch position is the climax of your journey back. Now, your weight is ready to come forward into the upswing of the U-shaped pendulum.

The landing position starts your weight shift forward. Landing on a closed front foot keeps your hips and shoulders on line with the ball.

After I've landed, my hands start down through the strike zone toward the contact position.

At contact, my arms are extended, my front leg is stiff, my hips are just about to open, and my back heel is off the ground so that my full power goes into the ball.

When you swing inside/out, your hands are in front of the bat barrel.

swing. Usually, I make contact just below the center of the baseball. This generates maximum underspin because it drives the ball faster and farther.

I like to hit the inside half of the ball using an inside/out swing with my hands ahead of the bat barrel. Inside/out swings produce gap shots and opposite-field line drives. However, I can still pull the ball with an inside/out swing when I make contact in front of the plate on the outside half of the ball. It all depends on where the ball is pitched and the point of contact along the path of my swing.

The inside/out swing requires patience to let the ball get in on you and is a major reason why I hit for such a high average. The inside/out stroke also maximizes your coverage of the outside corner when pitchers are working the inside and outside corners.

For mysterious reasons, most inside/out swingers are lefties. George Brett swings inside/out when he goes to left field. Rod Carew was the consummate inside/out hitter, and Tony Gwynn has a strong inside/out capability.

The alternative to the inside/out swing is the pull-hitter's swing. With the pull-hitter's swing, the bat barrel is ahead of the hitter's hands at contact and the hitter's hips are ahead of his hand set. Pull-hitter's swings usually produce hits up the middle or to the hitter's pull field. Ted Williams had the ideal pull-hitter's swing. The fact is, the pull-hitter's swing is the way most hitters attack the ball and the swing hitters use whenever they hit for full power.

The act of contact happens so fast, however, that my advice is simply to swing naturally through the ball. The longer you wait, the more likely it is that you'll make solid contact. But if your tendency is to hit the outside half of the ball with the pull-hitter's swing, stay with it. Above all, remember to keep your hips and shoulders closed as you approach the ball. Once you make contact, your body and the bat should go in an upward movement toward the finish.

THE FINISH

The pendulum is at its uppermost peak as you finish your swing—and you must finish *high* to lift the ball. If your mechanics are right, the finish is a silky follow-through that ends with your bat extending above your front shoulder.

If you've mastered the one-hand finish and can let go with your top hand at the precise moment of contact, you'll follow through with no resistance from your upper body. You'll get fuller arm extension and more punch on the ball. The reality, however, is that most players are taught to finish with two hands, and there may be more to lose by tampering with that than by keeping it. So, if you're a one-handed finisher, enjoy your edge, and if you're a two-handed finisher, stay that way. Hitting is hard enough without confusing yourself; and finishing a swing with two hands will never ruin a hitter's day.

When you use the pull-hitter's swing, the bat barrel's ahead of your hands on contact.

The one-hand finish is the friction-free way to complete your follow-through. Just let go with your top hand at the precise point of contact.

The two-hand finish is the traditional and most natural finish for most hitters. I always use it in games, and if you're comfortable with it, you should too.

AVOID A DOMINANT TOP HAND

One thing every hitter should always avoid is rolling the top hand over before contact. This so-called dominant top hand puts your hands in a weak hitting position at contact. Essentially, your bat arrives before the ball, and by the time the ball hits the bat you're into the finish of your swing. At best, you'll hit the top part of the ball for a line drive with topspin. At worst, you'll miss completely.

Dominant-top-hand swings can end up as hits, but they're the result of being fooled. To avoid them, recognize each pitch and distribute your weight slowly to the ball. Your hands should automatically roll over after contact as they head up to the finish of your swing.

Your wrists roll automatically after contact.

Keep your head still when you watch the ball and down on contact. Moving your head throws your body off the ball and prevents good contact.

KEEP YOUR HEAD QUIET

The quieter your head, the better you'll hit. A lot of hitters jerk their heads as they swing, causing them to tip or miss the ball. Moving your head throws your vision off the plane of the ball and takes your body and bat off track.

In a way, your head has the same effect on hitting that your feet have when you're chasing down fly balls. If you run on your heels, the ball seems to bob up and down with every step and is difficult to follow. But when you run on your toes, the ball doesn't change planes. You can judge where it's going a lot more clearly as you run, and it's a lot easier to catch.

When I bat, my head stays locked in a hitting position as if I were hypnotized by the pitch. My eyes move to pick up the ball, but the plane from which I view the pitch never changes.

George Brett is an expert at keeping his head still on every swing, which is another reason why he's such a great hitter. George's head points down on contact, but he never moves it while the pitch is en route because this keeps the rest of his body on line. The point is: Where your head goes, your body follows. So keep it still and make it the last part of your body to leave your swing.

DON'T LOSE SIGHT OF THE BALL

Pete Rose used to watch the baseball the way a hawk keeps an eye on its prey. There wasn't an instant when Pete's eye wasn't trained on the 3-inch sphere. He watched it when it hit the catcher's mitt, when the catcher threw it back to the pitcher, and when the pitcher rubbed it up while on the mound.

That kind of aggressiveness is one reason Pete had more hits than any other major-league player. He wanted the moment of contact more than other guys and went after it each at-bat, every game. Pete knew the adventure begins and ends with your eyes on that white object, and he fixed his on his target at all times. He never lost sight of the ball.

ONE EYE IS ALWAYS DOMINANT

Everyone has a lead, or dominant, eye that rules over the other when focusing on objects. Most people aren't conscious that this is so, but it is and I can prove it to you. Place a baseball on a table, set a chair 10 paces from the table, and sit down. Now, focus on the baseball with both eyes and line your index finger up directly between you and the ball. When your finger is blocking as much of the ball as possible, close one eye and keep the other fixed on the ball. Then repeat the process for the other eye.

You may be able to guess what's going to happen, but I'll tell you in advance. When you close your dominant eye, the baseball is going to look as if it moved left or right. When you close the other eye and your dominant eye is open, the ball is going to look as if it stayed in the same place.

What this all means is simple but important. Your dominant eye is the eye that you naturally rely on to tell you the location of objects—including ones in flight. When it comes to baseball, your dominant eye is the eye you want facing the pitcher, following the ball. Because the left eye is closer to the pitcher for right-handed hitters and vice versa, simple geometry dictates that left-eyed batters fare better as right-handed hitters and right-eyed batters fare better as left-handed hitters. You not only have a clearer, easier angle to view the ball when your dominant eye is out front facing the ball, you also won't be unconsciously turning your head or pulling out of your swing too soon to watch the ball.

I'm not suggesting that you switch sides of the plate if you discover you're not hitting with your dominant eye in front. However, if you have the time to experiment or if you're a young hitter just taking up the game, you may want to experience what it's like seeing the ball from your dominant-eye side. Take as many practice swings as you can and if you're dedicated, you may want to make a change.

Now that we've taken the swing apart, let's put all the pieces together in one fluid stroke. Start with your feet shoulder-width apart, your hands at or slightly below your chest, and your bat balanced in an upright, vertical position. Your weight is on the balls of your feet, evenly distributed on your front and back feet.

The trigger mechanism—in my case, the front leg—gets your swing started and your weight going back to 75–25 percent on your back foot.

The launch position puts you in a state of readiness to attack the ball. Your hands extend back to generate as much force as you need to come through the Impact Zone.

Landing on a closed front foot keeps your body on line with the pitch. Your weight is 50–50 percent front to back and you're ready to transfer the rest of your power through your front foot to the ball.

After you land, your front leg begins to stiffen so it can transport your power from your lower and upper body to the ball. Your hands and shoulders remain as they were in the launch position.

Your hands' journey to the ball begins with a downward movement from the landing position.

Your back leg bends and front leg stiffens to deliver your power to the ball. Your back foot automatically lifts as you finish your swing.

Your hands whip the bat through the Impact Zone as you transfer your weight to the ball.

Your head is down on contact. Your hips are about to open and your arms are extending slightly up to drive the ball. Your wrists roll automatically and your back foot is ½ to 1 inch off the ground.

Your arms continue to extend and your hips begin to open after contact. Your bat continues to head slightly up toward the finish of your swing.

Your hips and arms are fully extended as you head toward the finish. Your head remains down as if you had just made contact.

The high finish completes the pendulum, enabling you to get your full power into the ball.

In the end, your body is completely uncoiled and you're standing straight, ready to run to first base.

7

Glide Paths, Slumps, and Coaches

Hitting a baseball has never been trickier or required more skill. A batter has to gear up his swing to get around on fastballs and gear it down to hit the growing arsenal of off-speed pitches and hard breaking balls. Pitchers are forever trying to keep hitters off balance, and proper weight shift has never been more useful in keeping your swing on line.

As we have discussed, the trigger mechanism ignites your weight shift from front to back and gets your swing started early. Then, as you reach the landing position, you ride your weight from your back foot forward through your stiff front leg to the ball. But what happens if you're fooled? What can you do when you read fastball when what's coming is a slow curve? How can you adjust?

At this point, your hitting mechanisms are ahead of the pitch, but just how far ahead is the question. If your full weight has shifted, you're sunk. You're going to make very poor contact or miss because you can't slow down your swing to wait for the ball. But if you've still got weight left to transfer, you can adjust. That's why it's critical for every Conscious Hitter to have what I call a long *glide path.*

YOUR ANSWER TO GETTING FOOLED

The glide path is the time and space your bat travels through in the Impact Zone where you can make contact with the ball. It's governed by your ability to wait for every pitch and distribute your weight evenly to the ball. The longer your glide path, the quicker you can change gears to react to the spectrum of pitches from fastball to change-up.

The principle is much the same as lifting weights. In order to get the full benefit of each repetition, you need to expand and contract your muscles fully. In order to have a long glide path, you need to restrict and extend your swing fully through the Impact Zone. If your bat leaves the Impact Zone halfway through it, you're essentially cutting your swing in half. Your body is apt to pull away from the ball, and there's no slack left in your swing to make contact when it arrives.

Here, I've opened my hips early, put too much weight on my front foot, and am way in front of the ball. This hit's going to be a weak ground ball for an out because I don't have any slack left in my swing to power the ball.

Using a long glide path, however, maximizes your utilization and coverage of the Impact Zone, which dramatically increases your chances of making solid contact. You can follow each pitch longer and recover if you're fooled because you've still got weight left on your back foot to transfer to the ball.

Hitters who utilize three inches of the Impact Zone don't make very good contact because their bat exits the zone too soon. But if the arc of your swing spans 1½ to 3 feet into the Impact Zone, you're going to make great and consistent contact. Now, you can hit any pitch from the catcher's mitt to 2 feet in front of the plate.

The process begins as you estimate the point of contact based on your recognition of the pitch. Your brain tells you that contact will occur in a certain area of the Impact Zone, which becomes the bull's-eye for your bat. When you and your swing are right, you've beaten the pitcher and you're likely to get a hit. When you're wrong, however, you've been fooled and you're likely to make an out unless you can adjust.

The beauty of the long glide path is that it gives a hitter a second chance. You can create a new bull's-eye in the middle of a swing because you still have weight left to transfer from back to front and your hands haven't gone through the ball. Once your brain corrects its faulty message, your glide path simply adjusts in time to make contact for a hit.

The key is to control your weight shift by keeping your hands, shoulders, and hips back and your eyes fixed on the ball. If you let them go too soon, your bat will come through the Impact Zone too soon and too fast and you'll have nothing left on your swing to react to. However, if you have an increased glide path, you can stay in the Impact Zone longer and have time to react to a revised message to hit the pitch.

There are too many hitters who can't hit a change-up with a paddle because they have a short, quick glide path and can only hit a fastball. As a result, they get too far out in front too early. The bat goes through the Impact Zone before the ball arrives, and they're as good as out.

I'd be less than truthful if I told you I didn't get fooled, too, but there's a difference. In these cases, I know where the ball is heading, but my brain has misled me. I think the pitch is a fastball. I'm fooled: call it an optical illusion. Nevertheless, I maintain my hands and shoulders on the path of the ball. My hips stay closed. My head is still. My eyes move with the ball. I slow my swing and weight shift down. I allow the ball to catch up to my swing and, *bang,* I'm back on the track to contact because I still have slack left in my swing.

When I'm really fooled, this kind of contact can be flimsy—a foul or ground out. But often I adjust in time to hit a hard line drive. I remember Bert Blyleven once threw me a curveball that sent me nearly to the end of my rope, but I was still able to get enough weight behind my swing to hit it out of the park. That's what a long glide path can do.

Any time you see a hitter get a good stroke on an off-speed pitch after having swung at a fastball, he's either made a good guess or he's maximizing his coverage of the Im-

This time my weight's coming forward, but I'm waiting for the ball. My hands and shoulders are back in a good hitting position, and I'm about to explode into the ball.

pact Zone with a long, controlled glide path. Don Mattingly and Rod Carew have made careers by slowing down their swing to adjust to off-speed pitches; and with practice, you can too.

The key is to keep your front shoulder in and your hands back and wait as long as you can to ride your weight from back to front. If you're fooled, slow down your swing to get as much of your bat as possible on the ball. Stretching your glide path to the max may not always look pretty, but it's a great way to spoil a good pitch and minimize outs. Any time you can increase your hitting zone, the more chance you have to make contact and the more hits you'll get.

THE CHECK SWING

The check swing is another way you can use your glide path to shut down your swing when you're fooled—especially when you have two strikes or a strike you can't handle. Here, you're fighting to stay alive. If you let the pitch go, you're out. And if you swing, you're not going to make good contact.

Your goal is to foul the ball out of play and get another pitch to hit. The goal is to flick the bat to spoil the pitch and get another crack at a hit.

I've had countless times in my career when a check-swing foul ball with two strikes enabled me to draw a walk, get a hit, or drive in a run. In 1986, we were facing the California Angels in Game Two of the American League Championship Series. Mike Witt was on the mound for the Angels; I had two strikes with nobody

on base, and he threw a change-up which coaxed me into swinging too early. By the time the ball arrived, I had nothing left on my swing to attack the ball. I just flicked my bat and tapped a dribbler to third base for a hit. It wasn't pretty, but I got on base and Mike Witt didn't get the out he thought he deserved.

THE SLUMP: MENTAL, MECHANICAL, AND TOUGH LUCK

There are three types of batting slumps—mental, mechanical, and tough luck. Mental slumps are brought on by hitters who get down and start to doubt themselves. Mechanical slumps are caused by flaws in the swing, and tough-luck slumps are when you're hitting them where they are instead of where they ain't.

Sometimes no matter how well you're swinging, you won't have any hits to show for it—that's the worst kind of slump there is. Several times I've gone 0–8 over a couple of games and hit the ball hard six times. One night at Fenway in May 1989, for instance, I hit four of five shots against Shane Rawley of the Minnesota Twins and had just one hit.

That seemed to happen almost every night during the first half of the 1984 season. That was the worst slump I've ever had. I still managed to finish the year at .325, but everything I hit in April, May, and June was caught. During one four-game series in Oakland I went two-for-fifteen and could have had eleven hits. Oakland's outfielders made great plays on six line drives and—then—Oak-

The check swing can be a lifesaver when you're fooled and have two strikes on you.

land shortstop Alfredo Griffin gloved two ground smashes in the hole.

That was tough luck, and I felt terrible. But I learned a valuable lesson: Good swings don't always produce base hits. So, if you're swinging well and not getting hits, don't change a thing. Hold your head high, and your hits will fall. Also, don't give pitchers too much credit. So many times a hitter will go 0–4 and think he's lost it. If a pitcher like Frank Viola has an excellent change-up that makes you look silly, so be it. Don't give the next guy credit or wear yourself out taking extra batting practice. Each at-bat is a totally fresh experience. Don't let tough luck get you down. Remain the Conscious Hitter that you are, stay in your hitting cocoon, and keep swinging the bat.

The most dangerous slumps come from hitting ruts caused by breakdowns in mechanics and technique. If you go for a week with one or two hits, you're in a real slump, and you have to take a good look at your hitting checkpoints to see where you're going wrong.

These checkpoints are the individual pieces of the hitting puzzle that Conscious Hitters must maintain at all times—the movements that keep the swing in gear. They include your weight shift from start to finish and your upper- and lower-body mechanics that keep your swing in gear.

Use the chart below to help you right what's going wrong.

PROBLEM	CAUSE	SOLUTION
1. Striking out	Swinging at bad pitches	Be selective
2. Popping up	Front shoulder leaving early	Stay back
3. Flying out	Late contact	Start back early
4. Grounding out	Early contact/low finish	Slow down trigger mechanism
5. Squib shots	Head moving off ball	Keep head down
6. Soft liners	Indecisive swinging	Get aggressive
7. Choppers	Jerking upper body/ downswing	Finish high

YOU AND YOUR HITTING COACH

There's nothing like a hitting coach to help you filter out what works from what doesn't—especially when you're going bad. A good coach can not only teach you the fundamentals, he can also facilitate your adjust-ments and corrections, help you win games, and be a big boost to your confidence.

Walt Hriniak, who was with the Red Sox for many years, was a great asset. Walt and I had a special bond. He worked with me every day. He understood every aspect of my hit-

Walt Hriniak and I shared a special bond, but he'd be the first to tell you not to depend too much on your hitting coach. *Courtesy of The Boston Red Sox*

ting. He was like an extra set of eyes.

The thing to remember about your relationship with a hitting coach is that it has limits. Don't expect miracles from him, don't depend on him too much, and don't lean on him when you're at the plate. Too many times I've seen big leaguers in games looking toward the dugout for help from their hitting coaches when they should have been 100 percent focused on their at-bat.

A coach can teach you to hold and swing the bat a certain way, but if it doesn't feel right, you're not gaining anything. If you've got a big hitch in your swing and pitchers are beating you all time, you've got to get rid of the hitch. Your coach may say to keep your hands back, but you realize keeping your front shoulder tucked longer is your best solution. In this case, your best bet is to test your theory, explain it to the coach, and demonstrate it in batting practice. If he's a good one, he'll be proud that you took the initiative to solve your own problem.

Some hitting instructors might suggest a change in your style even if you're successful because they want something else out of your productivity. Ted Williams has always tried to coach me into opening up my hips sooner to pull the ball more when I'm ahead in the count. Naturally, whenever Ted Williams talks, I listen. But, frankly, opening my hips too early isn't comfortable for me and waiting longer for the ball is. So, I'm going to stick with my style because it works.

The truth is, not all the advice you get from a coach is going to be right for you, and not every coach is right. Players and coaches must try to show one another respect and listen to one another. But if your coach suggests something and you give it a good try in batting practice and games and it doesn't work, you've got to try something else. Mature hitters learn to follow their own advice. Smart hitters pay attention to their coach, test his advice, then make the final decision themselves.

8

The Power Curve: Contact Any Way You Want It

The Power Curve is the U-shaped arc your bat makes to and through the Impact Zone on every swing. Diagrammed, the Power Curve maps the bat's entire journey, tracing the pendulum of your swing from the launch position to contact, and so on. The curve varies on each pitch because your bat's route to the ball differs as to where the ball crosses the plate. I tend to think of it as a blueprint. It shows where along the path of my swing the bat hit the ball and explains why I hit a grounder, a line drive, or a fly ball.

The Power Curve also tracks the length of my glide path, how much of the Impact Zone I'm utilizing, and how well I'm shifting my weight. A flat, half-moon–shaped arc tells me I'm arriving late and finishing too low to utilize the front end of the Impact Zone. A steep V-shaped arc tells me I'm uppercutting, opening my shoulders too soon, or moving my head. (Hitters should never move their heads—only their eyes.) A perfect U-shaped arc tells me I'm shifting my weight just right, driving my bat and body directly to the ball, and extending my arms properly on the finish.

When I told Seattle Mariners' manager, Jim Lefebvre, about the Power Curve, he was amazed. Jim was the hitting coach for Oakland at the time, and Jose Canseco and Mark McGwire were his prize pupils. Jim knew the curve could help the two young sluggers, and he videotaped them at the plate. Then, he put a U-shaped transparency of the perfect swing on a TV screen and charted the curves of McGwire's and Canseco's swings as they stood against it. The exercise showed Canseco and McGwire the places along the Power Curve and Impact Zone where they hit best and helped them become two of baseball's best Conscious Hitters.

No one will ever drive a baseball exactly where and how he likes to every time—hitting's too tough. But the discovery of the Power Curve complemented by a proper swing and bat control enables hitters to produce the right hit in the right place at the right time. George Brett has been doing it for years. Rod Carew was one of the all-time masters, and Jose Canseco showed you can do it with power when he scattered his forty-one home runs in 1988.

The key to understanding how *you* can gain that kind of control begins by dividing the Power Curve into three basic contact areas: A–B, B–C, and C–D. The A–B zone is the first third of your U-shaped swing and occurs as your bat descends from your chest into the Impact Zone. The B–C zone is the middle third of the U and occurs as your bat levels through the heart of the strike zone. The C–D zone is the final third of the U and occurs as you start the up part of your swing toward your finish.

A–B contact usually occurs in the rear of the Impact Zone and produces hard ground balls or low line drives. Hitters like Jody Reed and Marty Barrett make their livings in the A–B zone, and it's the perfect area of the curve to utilize the hit-and-run. A–B hitters make contact on the down part of the slightly-up swing, which gives them a longer look to recognize each pitch. Hitting in the A–B zone is a big mistake when you need a sacrifice fly.

The A–B zone spans the first third of your swing as you sweep the bat on a downward path from your chest to the rear of the Impact Zone.

But if you have good speed and less-than-average power, it's a very effective way to get a hit or to advance a runner.

I've seen hitters when fooled or on tough pitches make contact on the downswing in front of the plate and hit the ball on the ground—sometimes for a hit. Technically, contact is made in the A–B Zone of the Power Curve. The trouble is, the downswing has been stretched too far by a premature weight shift and the hitter's arms have extended in a down position instead of slightly up. Far from the perfect U, the Power Curve on this swing looks like a C turned on its side. Often the hitter has taken a dominant-top-hand swing, and the finish is always very low. The ball may be hit fairly well, but never with the hitter's full force. Effective A–B contact takes place with your bat between the chest and belly button, not below the waist.

The second third of the curve, the B–C zone, is where I usually hit. The B–C zone is the maximum contact position because it produces hard line drives or gap shots. When you make B–C contact, your bat is at its flattest point at the heart of the Impact Zone

The B–C zone spans the middle third of your swing as your bat flattens through the heart of the Impact Zone.

and heading up. You can still hit a deep drive with height or a hard grounder, depending upon your point of contact on the ball. But most well-connected B–C hits are 10 to 20 feet off the ground—which is why B–C hitters are so difficult to defense.

B–C hitting gives you ample time to wait for the ball and recognize the pitch—but don't expect to slug forty home runs. Chances are you'll hit a line drive for a one- or two-base hit. Hitting consistently in the B–C zone is the main reason for my six batting titles and why I hit so many doubles up the power alleys. You won't find a better way to minimize outs.

C–D hitting usually takes place in front of the plate at the gateway of the Impact Zone closest to the pitcher. Contact occurs on the *up* part of the U-shaped swing, propelling the ball high and deep into the air. Your arms are fully extended, and 85 to 90 percent of your weight transfers directly to the ball on contact. When you want the long ball, C–D's the way to go, but it's not easy. Effective C–D hitting requires perfect timing and pinpoint accuracy.

The C–D zone spans the final third of your swing as your bat travels slightly up through the front of the Impact Zone toward the finish of your swing.

Your bat must travel a greater distance from the launch position to the ball, and total contact is required for full explosion and power. The trick is to recognize the pitch early, shift your weight quickly through the Impact Zone, then whip your bat to the ball without pulling your hips, head, and shoulders off the ball. Bat speed and body control are a must, which is why C–D hitting is so tough.

In lob ball or slow-pitch softball C–D hitting is relatively simple because the ball always comes at a slow rate of speed. Hitters have time to get to the front of the plate and no one worries about getting fooled. The flight of the ball in baseball, however, is a lot less predictable and requires a more disciplined response. If you're fooled, you've got little time to recover; and if you're hitting C–D, it's almost impossible to pull your weight back to correct your mistake. Granted, nothing feels better than C–D hitting when it works, but nothing looks more foolish when it doesn't. How many times did you see young Reggie Jackson fall off the right side of the plate after a big swing drew nothing but air?

Do you know that just about every high fly ball is a C–D swing gone sour? That's why the best way to hit C–D is to be selective—make sure you've got the pitch and power to go deep. You wouldn't throw the bomb every play of a football game. So, why do it in baseball? Let the C–D hits come naturally. Keep your glide path intact and open up early only when you're 100 percent sure you've recognized the pitch and you're going to crush the ball.

The reason Mike Schmidt and Henry Aaron—the greatest home-run hitter of all time—are two of the great C–D hitters alive is because each knew which pitch to hit C–D and when to go B–C. I ventured into the C–D zone quite a bit in 1987 when I hit twenty-four homers, but I was careful. I controlled my body and kept my bat in the Impact Zone until the ball arrived.

Generally, C–D hitters commit to one thing—dead red fastball. But I've seen plenty of successful C–D swings on hanging curves and poorly thrown change-ups. I've also seen ill-timed C–D swings produce a ground ball or a line drive on contact above the center of the ball. Believe it or not, you can also make C–D contact at the rear of the Impact Zone with an exceptionally short, quick swing. Your best bet, however, is to gear yourself to B–C and enter C–D only when you know you've got a pitch you can lift, like a fastball down the middle or a hanging curve. This gives you the best of both worlds and minimizes your mistakes.

HOW TO USE THE CURVE

Using the Power Curve can help a singles hitter like Chicago White Sox shortstop Scott Fletcher hit more home runs, and a home-run hitter like Mark McGwire hit more singles. You don't have to change your swing. It's a simple matter of adjusting your glide path along the curve to produce the hit you desire.

You don't need a video recorder or a camera, either. All you have to do is practice hitting in each of the three zones. Just use your glide path to control where you hit the ball in the

The toss-the-ball drill is a great way to learn to use the Power Curve. Here's a C–D smash into the net that would have gone deep to center field.

Impact Zone. Take ten to twenty swings in A–B, ten to twenty swings in B–C, and ten to twenty in C–D. Repeat the process during batting practice until you're comfortable in each hitting zone. Then apply it in games.

The "toss-the-ball" drill is another exercise you can use to sharpen and maximize your use of the Impact Zone and Power Curve. All you need is one friend, a protective net, and a backstop. The hitter sets up 10 to 12 feet in front of a backstop. The tosser kneels behind a net beside the hitter and flips baseballs along various points of the Impact Zone. The hitter then takes a series of ten swings in each zone of the Power Curve and to each field. Then the hitter and tosser trade places. This drill will really help you to change your sights and master your hitting zones along the curve.

Remember, the difference between a .250 and a .300 hitter over a 162-game season is one hit a week. I don't know how long your season is, but I can tell you this: The Power Curve can help. It sure worked for Spike Owen in spring training 1987.

My sights and weight are pointing the opposite way, and I'm letting the ball get in on me as I prepare to make this B–C contact for a line drive to left field.

Spike is a switch-hitting shortstop who hits line drives and an occasional home run, but sometimes made less than solid contact and ventured too much into C–D. First, I emphasized that he swing only at strikes. Then, I told him about the Power Curve and suggested he focus on B–C.

We also decided that Spike would strive for four more hits and two more walks than he got the previous spring, and that he'd bunt a little more and use his speed. Soon, Spike was shooting the sphere all over training camp. He finished with a .324 average, largely because the Power Curve helped him become smarter and more disciplined at the plate.

THE POWER CURVE IN GAMES

Whenever you step in the batter's box, you should already know what to do to help your team. Take a tie game in the last inning with two outs. In this case, you ought to be thinking C–D because a well-hit fly ball has a better chance of clearing the wall than a line drive. C–D hitting's also the choice when a man's on third with less than two outs. I call this playing with "house" money because so many good things can happen if I can vault the ball into the air.

The Power Curve can also help you hit to your strength because it explains where along the arc of your swing you hit best. If you're big and strong like Jose Canseco, you ought to look for pitches where you can take a C–D swing just as he does. Less powerful players like my teammates Barrett and Reed ought to stay in A–B or B–C, and hit the ball low and hard. What good's a C–D hit if you can't get it over the outfielders' heads?

The count and the ball park itself are also critical to using the Power Curve. In Yankee Stadium, for instance, if I'm up to two and one or three and two in the count, I can afford to go for a C–D shot to right field—where the fence is relatively short. If I want to pull the ball for a home run in Detroit, which also has a short fence, I recognize the pitch, shift my sights to right field, and make contact in the front part of the Impact Zone.

I don't change my stance or my swing. I simply shift my front shoulder and weight to the field and contact point that gets the job done. It's kind of like setting your hitting strategy on a sundial. To pull hit, make contact in front of the plate on the outside half of the ball. To hit up the middle, make contact in the middle of the plate in the center of the ball. And to hit to the opposite field, hit the ball on its inside half at any point along the Impact Zone.

The key is pointing your weight toward the ball and field where you want to hit and utilizing your glide path to get you there. If it were simple, we'd all hit .700. Sometimes you're going to get nasty pitches that come in very difficult spots. The higher you climb in baseball, the better the pitching and the more often you're going to see pitches that are very difficult to command.

If you get a sharp sinker inside, for instance, forget hitting the opposite way. Conversely, if you get a high, outside fastball, don't try to pull it. The angles just aren't working for you. Place the ball only on pitches you know you can handle—especially when there are two strikes on you.

Maximizing your use of the Power Curve will help you control pitches so that you can produce the hit you want. But nothing is perfect. No hitter has the advantage on every pitch. So, when you have a situation hit in mind, stay selective and remember to minimize outs. Only go after pitches that give you a good chance to accomplish your mission.

If you need a grounder, don't swing at a high pitch or commit your front shoulder to the ball until the last possible moment. If you need a fly ball, wait for a pitch high enough to hit in C–D. If you need to pull a line drive and are seeing low and outside pitches, get the bat out to the front of the plate and make contact in the B–C zone of your swing.

Again, change your sights, transfer your weight, and get started early so you *can* put the bat where it's needed to place the ball. One night at Fenway in 1985, lefty Britt Burns of the White Sox threw me an inside fast-ball that bore down on my hands. There was one out, a man on third, and I was thinking C–D all the way. Knowing what I had to do, I took an inside/out cut and doubled off the left-field wall to score the run. My hands came inside the ball with the bat barrel head ahead of them, enabling me to drive the ball to left rather than getting jammed. I also made contact in the rear of the Impact Zone and kept my weight back as I made contact in the high B–C part of the Power Curve.

You can do it, too. Just stay within the realm of your hitting style. If you have trouble hitting the other way, don't try it during a game. Work your Power Curve during batting practice. Study where your teammates make contact along the arc of their swing, and watch big leaguers' or college hitters' swings on TV. Knowing how to control contact will make you the best Conscious Hitter you can be.

WHERE BIG LEAGUERS HIT ALONG THE CURVE

Eric Davis: Eric tries to be in C–D all the time. He's very explosive, and—next to Canseco—probably has the best bat speed in the major leagues. Eric can generate so much explosive power that he can make a mistake and still hit the ball out of the park. He's one of the few hitters who can average .330 and hit forty home runs in a single season. Eric uses all fields and has excellent technique.

Jose Canseco: Jose has tremendous discipline and patience. He likes to wait for pitches and will walk if he doesn't get his pitch. His bat speed is so great he can get into C–D in a hurry, and he may be the most powerful man in baseball. Because Jose works hard to get his pitch and uses all fields, he can hit over .300 in any season. And because he knows how to wait for the ball, many of his best shots are hard-hit line drives originating in the B–C zone of the Power Curve.

Kirby Puckett: Kirby is pure aggression at the plate and the most successful free swinger in the big leagues. In 1988, he walked just twenty-nine times in over six hundred at-bats. There's no player who utilizes more of the Impact Zone, and no one does it in so many ways. Kirby can swing at balls 3 inches off the ground or 6 inches over his head and still get hits along every part of the Power Curve. Kirby is one of the few talents who violates the rules of good hitting and still succeeds.

9

Winning Hitting: Hard, Far, and Smart

Teams are a lot like my chicken dishes. Coaches whip up a lineup and if the recipe works, the team wins. In baseball, a winning mix is made up of multitalented hitters—each with a unique facet to his bat. Mike Schmidt could crush you with power, Rickey Henderson will beat you with speed, and Tony Gwynn will run you ragged all over the field. And that leads me to the first lesson of winning hitting: *No matter what kind of hitter you are, consistency is key.*

Earl Weaver used to say three-run homers win games, and they do. But one thing you don't need is a hitter who slams forty home runs, hits .210, and strikes out 180 times in 162 games. Too many times, those strikeouts squelch rallies, strand runners, and take you out of close games.

Dave Kingman was an awesome home-run hitter. His 442 round-trippers are nineteenth on the all-time list. He played in two All-Star Games and knocked in 1,210 runs. When Dave stepped in, pitchers watched their step or they watched Dave step around all four bases. Dave was powerful, all right, but I'm sure he'd be the first to tell you that he wasn't as consistent as he would have liked to have been.

In sixteen seasons, Kingman's .278 strikeout average was 42 points higher than his .236 batting average, and his on-base percentage was just .305. And yet, can you imagine what he would have done had he minimized his outs? Sure, he might have belted twenty instead of thirty home runs every season, but his average could have climbed to .275 or .280, his RBI total might have gone up fifteen or twenty a year, and he would have had many more game-winning hits and runs scored. Dave Kingman would have been a whole lot more productive.

HIT AS HARD AND AS FAR AS YOU CAN

A home run is *the* prestige hit in the game, and you won't score any faster. The trouble with the home run has nothing to do with the homer itself. It's the myth that home-run hitters drive Cadillacs and singles hitters drive Volkswagens that bothers me; and it filters down through every tier of organized baseball.

I can still remember two minor-league managers coming down on me for not hitting enough home runs when my average was well above .300. But what gets me is when the home-run mentality trickles down to Little Leaguers. If a kid goes two for four with a single and a double every day and hits three home runs in a twenty-game season, he's done the job. And he's done it well. Home runs come when you've hit the ball in the right place at the right time. Don't force 'em.

If I could hit sixty-one home runs every season, I'd roll over; but the fact is, it's not a high-percentage hit. Look at the statistics. The average number of American League home runs in 1988 was nineteen, or only 2 percent of 650 times at bat. Even Jose Canseco, the league leader, had only forty-two. Jose was up 610 times, so even the very best home-run hitter in 1988 hit a home run 7 percent of the time—only 7 of every 100 times up.

Half of Canseco's homers may have won ball games for the A's—no question, they're important. The other half, however, may have come when games were already won or lost and meant relatively little. Ask yourself: If Jose's home-run swinging knocked forty or fifty points off his .307 average, would the home runs be worth the cost? Of course not. Jose's base hits sustain rallies and drive in runs, and he'd have to adjust his swing to minimize outs.

Reggie Jackson, one of the game's all-time great sluggers, geared himself to hit home runs, and he smashed some of the most titanic shots I've ever seen. When Reggie stood in the batter's box, he had one thing on his mind: muscle the inside fastball into the right-field seats. Yet, late in his career as his power waned, he changed his style and began using the whole field. If he got an inside fastball, he still hammered it deep to right, but he also began driving outside pitches to left and hitting liners to the gaps. Reggie got a lot smarter in his final days and prolonged his career long after he had reached his home–run–hitting prime.

If you want to hit home runs, Henry Aaron's career teaches the best lesson I know. Hank showed you could hit homers by being selective. He was the greatest technique home-run hitter who ever lived. For years, Hank was a line-drive hitter who went with every pitch. As he got older, however, he began hitting choice pitches in front of the plate and driving the ball higher and deeper in the air. Hank wasn't big and strong like Frank Howard or Harmon Killebrew. He didn't hit 500-foot monster shots. His home runs were the result of hitting the right pitch in the right place, and usually he hit them just far enough. His 715th record-breaking home run exemplified that. It just cleared the fence before Hank's teammate Tom House caught it in the bullpen.

My ideal power hitter hits twenty-five home runs, has a .340-to-.350 batting average, and drives in 100-plus runs. That's why I think George Brett has been baseball's most productive hitter for the past several years. George seldom strikes out, he can hit a rope (a hard line drive) to any part of the ball park, and he's as likely to hit the homer as anyone in the game. George may not be the most powerful power hitter, but he's the most consistent—and that's what counts.

Personally, I try to put the fat part of the bat barrel on the choice part of the ball—just underneath its center. And *I hit the ball as hard and as far as I can.* If I hit a home run, great, but my job is to minimize outs, so I usually hit line drives to the right- and left-center-field gaps: the biggest part of every ball park—some 380 to 420 feet away. As a result, most of my best shots are doubles rather than home runs, and I'll take 'em any time because they set up or drive in runs.

THERE'S POWER THE OPPOSITE WAY

Talk about hitting the opposite way, and people think of weak singles dropped over the infield. Nothing could be further from the truth. Arguably, scratch hits will forever be part of baseball, but opposite-field hitting is not scratch hitting—it's smart hitting.

Opposite-field hitting enables you to use the whole field and makes the defense play you honestly.

First, opposite-field hitting enables you to use the whole field and makes the defense play you honestly. Second, it allows you to wait a drop longer to diagnose the pitch. And third, you can hit the ball just as hard and almost as far with good contact.

Jose Canseco hits home runs to the opposite field. Jim Rice did it for years, and I've put a few in the left-field screen at Fenway Park over the years. It's almost like a backhand in tennis. You won't get as full a finish or as much power hitting opposite your strong side, but you can still make contact in front of the plate and clear a 370-foot fence. And you can still get extra-base hits.

Many of my league-leading doubles in 1988 were gap shots to left center that outfielders couldn't track down despite playing me that way. This approach worked wonders for my average and helped my team. I don't always go up to the plate planning to go to the other field. I wait long enough to recognize the pitch and take my natural swing.

Writers have often asked me why I don't pull more, so let's explain. Suppose Jack Morris throws a fastball and I pull it hard but foul to right field. Great swing, I say to myself, ready to attack Morris again. The next pitch I get out in front again, but whoops, it's a fork ball and I ground out to second.

Say the next time up, Morris starts me with a fastball down the middle. I'm out in front again and foul it off—another good swing. Then he throws a change-up, I get out in front again, but this time I hit a weak grounder off the end of the bat to shortstop Alan Trammell, who throws

me out. Now I'm 0 for 2.

On my third trip I decide to wait a millisecond longer. This time Morris throws a fastball inside, and I line it to right field. Base hit. The next time up, I get the fork ball and I drive it to left center, hit the gap for a double. Now I'm two for four.

Remember: The wisdom of opposite-field hitting lies in doing it selectively. All you need to do is let the ball get in on you, then make contact in whatever mode along the Power Curve that suits your objective.

WHATEVER HAPPENED TO THE HIT-AND-RUN?

The hit-and-run became a lost art when teams went to base-stealing leadoff hitters like Rickey Henderson and Vince Coleman. But it's still a great play that dictates the defense and can win ball games if the right man is at the plate.

If you're up, your first move is to check who's covering second as the runner from first takes off. If the second baseman covers, hit to right. If the shortstop covers, hit to left. Either way, wait as long as you can before you swing, keep your front shoulder down, and make A–B contact.

Be sure you keep the ball on the ground and remember your first priority: contact. Also, keep the ball away from the middle of the infield where the pitcher and infielder covering second are waiting. It's better to swing early or late. A line drive is great if you get a hit because the runner goes to third, but your job is to advance him in the safest way possible. A–B through the hole in the infield's the way.

Marty Barrett has a natural A–B stroke and is an excellent hit-and-run batter. He's quick to see who's covering the bag and makes reliable contact. Willie Randolph is another good contact hitter who can do the job. He knows how to hit the ball on the ground and can hit it hard where he wants to.

THE BUNT: SINGLES, SETUPS, AND SACRIFICES

Bunting is an important part of baseball that big-league teams don't take enough advantage of. Third and first basemen usually line up so deep on the diamond that most players could skip down to first base if they just put the ball down. Yet only a few crafty batsmen like Rod Carew and the legendary Ty Cobb have used the bunt as a weapon. These great hitters had the sense to bunt for base hits and force the defense to play them honestly. Then, when the infield cheated in to protect against the bunt, they'd hammer the hard ground ball or line drive through the infield for a base hit.

Red Sox second baseman Marty Barrett is another good bat handler who knows how to use the bunt. Marty can lay the ball down with the best of them, and he's learned to use the bunt to set up other plays. With runners on first and second and less than two outs, Marty can fake the bunt, forcing the shortstop to cover third base, then hit the ball through the shortstop hole for a hit. What a great way to minimize outs and drive in runs.

Beating out a bunt *isn't* just as good as a hit, it *is* a hit. And sacrifice bunts are a big part of winning hitting, too, especially when you're playing for one run late in the game. An effective sacrifice bunt advances the runner and puts tremendous pressure on the defense. How many times have you seen infielders bobble bunts or rush themselves into a bad throw on a good bunt? It sure happens in the big leagues. So, be smart. Don't ignore bunting—master it. Practice it with the same zeal that you practice your swing.

When preparing to bunt, position the bat 45 degrees in front of the plate in fair territory with your knees slightly bent. As the ball is delivered, bring the bat down so that it's perpendicular to the plate. Balls bunted in the rear of the Impact Zone typically go foul behind the plate because your arms and hands are coiled in a weak bunting position. Instead, set yourself in the front of the Impact Zone and push your hands and arms into the pitch. Sometimes the defense knows you're in a bunting situation and will cheat in, but if they're not on to you, don't tip them off until you get a good pitch. Always try to get it right the first time.

There are two basic styles of laying down a sacrifice bunt. One way is to pivot on the balls of your feet or square as the pitcher goes into his windup. In each case, however, the idea is to deaden the ball on contact as if there were a glove on the end of your bat to retrieve and roll the ball back slowly in play. Make the first or third baseman field the ball and keep

They won't throw me out on this "pivot-style" bunt. My feet are lined up one in front of the other. My bat's right in front of the plate, and I'm rolling the ball from the sweet spot 10 to 12 feet down the line.

Squaring allows you to put the bat on the ball in a fully balanced position. Keep your legs side by side, with your weight on the balls of your feet so that your eyes stay on the same plane as the ball.

MARTY BARRETT

Marty Barrett is a sure bet to bunt the ball down when the team needs a sacrifice, and he knows how to fake the bunt and drive the ball past the charging or shifting infield.
Courtesy of The Boston Red Sox

it away from the pitcher. The pitcher always has the easier throw, no matter which base the lead runner's going to.

The ideal bunt goes about 5 to 8 miles per hour, roughly 10 to 12 feet on the ground. Be mindful to lay off high pitches that produce pop-ups. The last thing you want when bunting is a ball hit into the air for a sure out or a double play if the base runner can't get back to the base on time. This is especially important on the squeeze play, where the runner on third is heading full speed toward the plate once the pitcher releases the ball.

Another thing to look for is how the pitcher falls off the mound on his follow-through—whether he's balanced enough to field the ball and which side is toughest for him to cover. If you're a lefty like me and the pitcher falls off to the third-base side, you've got a nice little lane to push the ball through between the mound and the first-base line for a sacrifice or a hit.

Sacrifice bunting won't hurt your average and is one of the most appreciated plays in the game. Ever notice the number of high-fives you get when you lay down a bunt that advances a runner? Teammates are grateful that you've given yourself up for their sake. So, don't moan or groan when the coach gives you the sacrifice sign. That's your job, and you should do it as enthusiastically as when you're swinging for a hit.

When you're bunting for a hit, you have two choices. One is to come to the ball with your back foot trailing your front foot piggyback style. The other way is to drag the ball toward your pull side of the infield. Either way is effective, but remember to recognize the pitch before committing yourself to it. Your glide path isn't the same U-shaped arc as when you swing, but you've got to keep your lower and upper body on line to the ball en route to the Impact Zone. So, take the rules of Conscious Hitting with you whenever you bunt for a hit, squeeze, or square.

PLAY THE ELEMENTS: THE VALUE OF STAIRWAY HITTING

The elements have an effect on every game and every player; and players have good and bad months based on weather. In Florida where I grew up, it's warm and sunny all year, and that's when I hit best. Bundle me up in the cold New England spring and I'll still get my bat on the ball; but June, July, and August—they're the months for me.

In April, I usually hit .305 to .315. In May, I probably hit .330, and in June I'm apt to hit .350. In July, I'm around .370, and in September I can reach .390. Then, as the weather cools in early October, I might drop to .350 or .360. If we're in the play-offs or World Series, I get enough adrenaline going to keep warm and work extra hard to keep the snowball rolling.

The point is, hitters are battling the environment as well as their opponents—even when playing indoors. Take Fenway in April. It can be 35–40 degrees with the wind blowing in from the outfield. In more temperate times, if I hit a good C–D shot to left field, I can hit the wall. But in

April, the wind holds the ball up, and I'll fly out. So, in this instance, I strive for B–C contact toward the right-field line. Just like that, I'm a pull hitter.

When it starts warming up in mid-to-late May and the wind blows out to center field, I'm back in the C–D range gunning for the wall. That's what Stairway Hitting is all about. Go up the stairs of the Power Curve when the wind is blowing out and down the stairs when it's blowing in. Know when to play the ball high and when to play it low.

TURF AND GRASS

Astroturf is another element that's crept into baseball at the college and professional level. The speed with which balls soar up the carpet causes infielders to play deeper, enabling them to cover more ground and cut off a lot more balls. On the plus side, when the infield's in on the turf, the hard ground ball's going to go through faster than on grass. But that's your only advantage.

Grass is my favorite surface because it slows down ground balls heading toward the hole and makes it tougher for the shortstop's throw to beat a hustling runner to first. Grass is also more pleasing to my eyes and stays cooler in hot, steamy weather.

10

The Pitcher's Tools: Recognizing Each Pitch

There are two ways pitchers get hitters out. One way is by moving the ball inside and outside across the width of the plate. The other way is by changing speeds along the 60-foot, 6-inch highway between the mound and the hitter.

When a pitcher works inside/outside, he's slicing the plate in sections, committing his pitch to a specific area, and gambling that if he gets the ball there you won't get a hit. When a pitcher works 60 feet, 6 inches, he's moving the ball up and down the strike zone using off-speed and breaking pitches. In each case, however, his goal is the same: to keep you off balance and exploit your trouble spots.

Tom Seaver was a 60-foot, 6-inch man who knew how to get people out. I faced him after his prime when he'd lost some steam off his fastball—but he was crafty. Seaver threw three different fastballs with different speeds, including one at batting-practice speed. He had two curves—a sweeping curve and a tumbler—which he threw from different release points, and a very nasty change. He could really fool you, and his delivery was always the same so you couldn't tell what was coming. Talk about keeping hitters off balance.

Oakland's Matt Young, a lefty, is an inside/outside specialist. Matt's got an overpowering fastball that can sail in or away from left-handed hitters. You just never know where it's going. Matt also has a nice break on his curve and a sharp-breaking slider to work the corners.

Knuckleballers like Charlie Hough are the cagiest 60-foot, 6-inch hurlers alive. Knuckleballs never do the same thing twice. The knuckler is the single toughest pitch to control and the hardest to hit because no one—including the pitcher—knows where it's going.

All pitchers throw in sequences, and their weapon is surprise. When it comes to a fastball situation, they might throw a change-up. When they think you're guessing curve, you're apt to see a slider. If the defense is playing you to pull, expect to see pitches on the inside part of the plate.

Tom Seaver threw three different fastballs at three different speeds.
Courtesy of The Boston Red Sox

If the defense lines up toward the opposite field, expect pitches on the outside part of the plate.

Once a pitch is past, forget it. Get ready for the next pitch. Don't try to get out more quickly on the next pitch if you just saw a fastball or gear your next swing down because the last pitch was a change-up. Remember, swinging *through* the ball gives you the plate coverage to hit any inside or outside pitch, and your long glide path allows you to adjust to changing speeds.

So, forget what happened with the previous pitch and focus on what's ahead. You don't have to guess—because once you learn to recognize the pitch, you'll know what's on the way when the ball's five feet out of the pitcher's hands.

RECOGNIZING EACH PITCH

The faster you recognize each pitch, the more quickly you can react and the more bat control you have to hit where you like. My goal is to make that assessment in a microsecond within 5 to 10 feet of the pitcher's release. If Matt Young throws a curve and I take a fastball swing, I'm in trouble. My weight is going to come forward too fast, and my bat's going to enter and exit the Impact Zone too soon to make good contact. Most likely, I'll hit the top half of the ball and ground out to short—all because I didn't recognize that pitch.

Granted, a long glide path will buy you extra time to adjust, but no hitter can hit a pitch he misjudges no matter how well he shifts his weight. However, if Matt throws that same curve and I read it, I can shift my weight properly and make the kind of contact that satisfies my hitting situation.

If you learn to recognize each pitch, not only will you know what's coming, you'll also know where the ball's going and whether it's going to be a strike. This skill is not too hard to learn. The first step is to focus on the pitcher's release point—the imaginary box above his head where he discharges the ball. Then, all you have to do is read a few simple keys regarding the spin or dominant color of the approaching pitch. Here's what to look for and how to hit each pitch.

The Curve: The curveball always goes up as it leaves the pitcher's hand, then loops down over the plate. The pitcher snaps the ball on the release, creating centrifugal force in a vacuum, which causes the ball to break down. The key to recognizing the curve, however, isn't the spin. It's your eyes.

When it's a curve, your eyes bob reflexively up then down in response. This usually occurs within 5 to 8 feet of the pitcher's release point as the ball changes from a higher to lower plane on its way down. Once you read the curve, rely on your glide path to shift your weight properly into the Impact Zone. If you're fooled, change hitting lanes by downshifting your swing to allow the ball to catch up to your bat.

Fastball: The fastball spins backward from the bottom up and is the easiest pitch to read. Usually, fastballs tail into like-handed and away from opposite-handed hitters, but the color is always pure white because only two of the baseball's four seams

Bruce Sutter is the father of the fork ball, and the fork ball is a big reason why, today, pitchers have an edge. *Courtesy of The St. Louis Cardinals*

are visible. When you know it's a fastball, shift into overdrive and hit to your strength.

Slider: The slider is faster and takes a sharper, more sudden break than the curve. The slider moves 6 to 8 inches from right to left when thrown by a right-handed pitcher and vice versa. It looks like a fastball, but is easily distinguished by a prominent red dot which stands out as the ball spins toward the plate.

The slider can be tough against like-handed pitchers as it darts inside to outside and is a good pitch to hit the opposite way against like-handed pitchers. The slider breaks into you against opposite-handed pitchers and is a good pitch to pull. The key in each case is the red dot. Once you see it, it's your pitch to handle.

Fork ball (split-finger fastball): Reliever Bruce Sutter probably locked up a spot in baseball's Hall of Fame when he invented the fork ball in the mid-seventies, and it's as tricky a pitch as you'll see. The fork ball has the same arc and speed as a fastball as it tumbles en route to the plate before the bottom falls out like a flat tire. The tip-off to the fork ball comes in the red/white, red/white spin as the pitch starts to tumble. The key to attacking it is patience. Keep your bat in the Impact Zone long enough to go with the pitch.

Change-up: The change-up is thrown with the same arm speed as the fastball, and is just as white on sight. Sometimes a pitcher will tip it off in his delivery or grip, but by and large your best answer to the change is a long glide path. The longer you stay back on the ball and keep your shoulders on line, the less effective the pitch is going to be. The change-up, more than any other pitch, is why the long glide path was invented and why it's a necessity when hitting a baseball.

Knuckler: A knuckler is by far the toughest pitch to hit because you don't know where it's going. Some of the balls that Charlie Hough throws even rise—which seems to defy every gravitational law I know. As with the change-up, you have to wait until the last possible second and let the ball come to you. You can't go out in front of the plate because the ball can skip at the last second, and then you're done.

Usually, you know a knuckler's coming because you're facing a knuckleball specialist. My former teammate Al Nipper, however, was not a strict knuckleballer and mixed it into his repertoire of pitches. In this case, the pitch wasn't as predictable, but you could recognize it because it wiggled a few feet out of the pitcher's hand and always came in slowly.

Sinker: Sinkers trick hitters just enough to get them to top the ball and hit it on the ground. You're never really fooled in the classic sense of pulling your body off line. Instead, hitters usually commit themselves to a contact point just above the actual location where the ball crosses the plate.

Sinkers usually go into lefty hitters from right-handed pitchers, and vice versa. This pitch comes at you with sliderlike speed, then dovetails at the last second. There's no tip-off to the drop, but if you stay in your hitting cocoon, you can still get a good piece and hit a hard line drive. Your best bet is to force the pitcher to throw the sinker up—and if it hangs, watch out. You may be taking a very quick trip around the bases.

Screwball: Willie Hernandez and Fernando Valenzuela have won Cy Young awards with the screwball. The screwball looks just like a curveball and will cause your eyes to bob. The difference is the spin. Whereas the curve spins to the opposite side that the pitcher throws from, the screwball spins to the same side. Thus, Willie's and Fernando's screwballs come into me and away from right-handed hitting Dwight Evans or Jim Rice. Don't expect to see many of these unusual pitches, but when your eyes bob and the spin goes in reverse of the curve, the screwball's on the way.

Spitball: There are two things we all know about the spitball. First, it's illegal; second, pitchers throw it just the same. Sometimes they'll hide

Gaylord Perry greased the ball better than anyone and got away with it for years. He was one of the great ones with and without it. *Courtesy of The San Francisco Giants*

Vaseline or baby oil on the inside of their pants or beneath their cap or glove. Other times, they'll sneak some saliva or sweat onto their hands to doctor the ball. Then, the catcher wipes off the wetness when the ball is called for inspection by a suspicious ump.

Gaylord Perry finally got caught throwing the spitter in a game in Seattle late in his great career, and Jay Howell was suspended for two games in the 1988 National League Championship Series for sneaking pine tar into his glove. The spitter itself squashes out of the pitcher's hand with fastball spin, then collapses across the plate like a fork ball. Your glide path will protect you once again, but the path of least resistance is to tell the ump.

GUESS HITTING: A GAMBLE YOU DON'T HAVE TO TAKE

Guess hitting is anticipating the pitch before you see it. This is something you don't need to do. A hitter may be waiting for a 2–2 slider, a 2–1 fastball, or a 1–2 curveball. He's psyched the pitcher and made his estimation. His focus is on one pitch, and he's ready for one pitch only. A right guess and he's got a good chance for a hit; a wrong guess and he's likely to swing and miss.

I don't guess because I don't have to; I can recognize each pitch and I start early enough and stay back long enough to hit whatever's coming. And what if a pitcher throws four different pitches? I've got a 75 percent chance of being wrong.

The odds get even slimmer against a guy like Jack Morris. He's got five pitches: a curveball, slider, change, and a fork ball to go along with his heater (fastball). If I guess Morris is coming with a 2–2 fork ball and he throws a fastball, I'll never catch up to it, and I'm going to swing and miss.

Guessing worked in Ted Williams's time because pitchers usually had only two pitches: a fastball and a curve. When a hitter got ahead 2–0, pitchers would invariably throw the hard one. So guessing fastball made sense. The trouble with guessing began with the use of the slider in the fifties and sixties. The slider looked just like a fastball until it swept across a corner of the plate. Right-handed pitchers would jam left-handed hitters and get right-handed hitters to miss on pitches low and away. Even Ted had trouble with the slider. He was so set on mastering it, he had a friend throw him sliders in his backyard until he learned to hit them.

Guessing became more difficult in the mid-seventies when Bruce Sutter developed the fork ball. The fork ball looked just like a fastball and fooled hitters as the slider had. Today, every pitcher's got a fork ball, which makes guessing even more likely to be wrong.

Instead of guessing, think fastball. Thinking fastball gears you up to handle the hard one, and you can still gear down to hit the off-speed and breaking pitches using your long glide path. This way, you can hit whatever's coming and there's no need to play the guessing game.

If you're a Little Leaguer, most pitchers are going to throw nothing but fastballs. In this case, your first rule is to swing at strikes. The ball's not going to change planes in flight, it's just going to come in inside and outside. Just wait for your pitch and go after it.

HITTING LIKE-HANDED PITCHERS

Facing a pitcher throwing from the same side that you hit from presents a different release point and flight path. Fastballs come at inside and away instead of outside and in. Breaking balls also go away instead of toward you. Many hitters get thrown off balance or tied up by the geometric change—but you can beat it.

The key is staying back and making sure you don't open up too soon. Once again, keep your front side in and your shoulders and hips on the ball. Stay in your hitting cocoon and take your ordinary stride to the ball. You don't have to make any other mechanical changes. Keep in mind the fact that the pitcher still has to throw a strike across the 17-inch dish. And remember, once you recognize the pitch, you've got the skills and know-how to drive the ball.

11

My All-Star Lineup: What Each Spot Should Accomplish

Making out a lineup is like putting a bunch of actors on a stage without a script. The director, in this case the manager, chooses his cast and when they appear—but he never knows what's going to happen. The best he can do is assess what to expect from each player and what he wants from each of the nine spots in the batting order.

In my book, your first two hitters are your best bat handlers and base runners: the setup men for your big guns. The number-one hitter should be a speed burner who has a high on-base percentage and swings at strikes. Your number-two man should be able to advance number one with a sacrifice bunt or hit-and-run. He needs to use the entire field and make consistent contact on every swing.

Number three is the best all-around hitter on the team. He's going to spray the outfield with base hits and long drives. When he gets on, number four's got to drive him in and anyone else he left on base. Number five has got to continue the rally or

drive number four in. He's also going to be a good contact hitter who takes the base on balls to set up number six. Number six is pure power. He's your mop-up man and the team's freest swinger. When number six unloads, it's time to clear the bases. I'm talking home run all the way.

Numbers seven, eight, and nine are often undervalued, but they're your lineup's winning edge. Don't ever forget: They're one-third of your order. They need to produce, and each plays a role just as important as the members of the front six. Number seven has to be a good contact hitter. His job is to fuel the rally in progress or get things going again. Number seven should be able to spray the ball across the entire field and take it deep from time to time. Number eight ought to be a heavy hitter who can hit the hard line drive and make you pay the home-run way if you make a mistake. Power from the number-eight spot is a big plus, when number seven's on base; and when your team needs a sacrifice fly, he's the one who ought to deliver. Number eight requires more punch than speed—particularly if you've got the right man stationed at number nine.

There are few hitters who can spark a rally like number nine. The ninth hitter is like a second leadoff man. His job is to run, walk, or hit his way on base, and he should also be ready to bunt. A good number-nine hitter is going to give your front four a lot more opportunity to do their stuff, and is a great asset to the team.

Because your lineup demands productivity from every spot, sometimes you've got to shake it up. Hitting can be a roller coaster of ups and downs, and players respond differently. Some players are going to hit better when moved back in the order when they're struggling. Others are going to get hotter if they move up when they're doing well.

Occasionally, an entire team can go into a slump that causes the order to need fixing. Red Sox manager Joe Morgan did it in the 1988 play-offs. We'd lost two straight games to Oakland, 2–1 and 4–3, in which we scored just four runs. So, the next game, Joe moved me from leadoff to third. He shifted Ellis Burks from fifth to leadoff and Dwight Evans from third to fifth. We lost 10–6, but at least the new-look lineup produced runs, and I give Joe a lot of credit for making the change.

I must admit, I've seen a lot more American League than National League hitters. But if I had to take nine to Olympic or world competition, the players below each have earned a spot on my card. Here's why I chose them.

1. **Rickey Henderson:** Rickey is one of the most potent leadoff hitters I've ever seen. He's one of the fastest men in the game. He's proven he can reach base 42 percent of the time and he can steal 80 to 100 bases a year. Rickey's good for 50 RBIs a season and he'll score 130. He has a good eye, is very selective, and has more than sufficient power—no one in baseball has led off more games with home runs. Rickey is also a solid stay-back hitter who doesn't overcommit himself to the pitch. B–C to C–D.

2. **Rod Carew:** Rod was never afraid to do business with two strikes and is the perfect man to advance Rickey Henderson. He can hit anywhere from .320 to .380 and will score 110 runs in the process. Rod can hit the gaps, shoot it through the infield, or beat out a drag bunt or fake the bunt and line by the defense. B–C.

3. **George Brett:** George is a super contact hitter and the right man to continue the rally. At his best, George averaged .390 and can hit thirty-five home runs. He's a 100-plus RBI man, who seldom strikes out and is always tough in the clutch. George will get Rickey and Rod in scoring position with less than two outs and he can hit forty doubles because he uses the whole field. George can hit the hard ground single up the middle, the long fly ball over the fence, or the line drive to the gaps. He gets it up in the air when he wants to and knows how to handle the full arsenal of pitches. B–C, C–D.

4. **Mike Schmidt:** Mike is pure power. He can hit thirty-five to forty home runs and still average a solid .270 despite swinging in C–D all the time. He's got the punch to knock in 110 to 120 runs, and he's selective.

Mike Schmidt of the Philadelphia Phillies. *(Copyright© 1988 Ed Mahan Photo)*

At his best, Mike can deliver a .650 slugging average, and when you're looking to clear the bases, he's got the bat I want on the ball. C–D all the way.

5. Dwight Evans: After Mike's cleared the bases, Dwight's the man for the job. Dwight forces the pitcher to deliver the pitch he wants or he trots to first base with a walk. He can give you thirty home runs, 100 RBIs and hit right around .300. At number five, I want Dwight to start another rally or back Mike up with power and consistently good contact. Because he's got good power, he is apt to hit into the air and doesn't strike out much. Dwight's the one to help the cause. High B–C.

6. Tony Armas: Tony is a classic powerhouse who can hit forty-plus home runs and average .300 at his best. Tony swings in one gear only— up, up, and away. And when he connects, forget it. If Mike and/or Dwight is on third base with less than two outs, Tony's going to hit high and deep enough to score them. But he can also do damage on his own. Tony's going to strike out more than Dwight or Mike because he takes a bigger swing. The good news is, he's

Tony Armas of the California Angels. *Courtesy of The California Angels*

got the bat control to make monstrous contact a good portion of the time—and when he's up, opposing pitchers are very, very careful. C–D all the way.

7. Harold Baines: Harold's got the stick I want to renew my rally. His bat is exceptionally quick. He's a .290 hitter who can crack forty doubles and twenty-plus home runs, and he can drive in 80 to 100 runs if Dwight and Tony are getting on base. Harold also has the speed to bunt if the defense is giving it away, and he makes steady, reliable contact. B–C, C–D.

8. Frank White: Frank's a favorite to any fan who appreciates a well-conditioned, self-made athlete. Frank is as well-rounded a hitter as you can find for number eight. He makes great contact, walks, and can give you a .300 on-base percentage. Frank also has better than average speed and can hit twenty-plus home runs. You won't find anyone more mentally or physically tough. B–C. Sometimes C–D.

9. Scott Fletcher: Scott's the best pre-leadoff hitter I know. He's got speed and can steal ten to fifteen bases a year. He strikes out under sixty times a season and he'll average .270–.280. Scott can get himself into scoring position in a hurry, and you can count on him to break up the double play. He knows how to work the count to get his pitch. He's got a good work ethic at the plate and is the type of team player who can fulfill the number-nine hitter's special role. A–B, B–C.

Catcher Carlton Fisk is over forty and would have retired years ago if he hadn't kept himself in such great shape. *Courtesy of The Boston Red Sox*

12

Diets, Workouts, and Superstitions: Building a Power Package That's Here to Stay

I've often wondered what hurts worse: injuries or not playing because of them. I've missed only a handful of games so far in my career, but every one was painful. The fact is, I play baseball because I love baseball, and when I'm sidelined with a muscle pull or tendinitis, the ache is more than physical.

Conditioning also affects your hitting. You don't just hit with your arms and hands. You hit with your total body, and the more power you generate from your feet up, the harder you can drive the ball. That's why I look at my body as a power package and do my all to be as strong and resilient as possible.

Fortunately, advances in nutrition, training, and medical technology are a big help to us all. Today, well-conditioned players can stay in the big leagues longer than ever. Two of baseball's best catchers—Carlton Fisk and Bob Boone—are both over

forty, and Nolan Ryan at forty-three looks as young as ever. But these athletes didn't just depend on doctors and trainers to patch them up. They developed solid workout programs to stretch and strengthen their muscles. And if you want your body to stand up to the stresses and strains of playing every day, you need to work out too.

Youngsters ten or eleven years old should begin stretching and weight training, but they must be closely supervised by coaches or health-club counselors. Usually kids get enough cardiovascular work riding their bikes and playing with friends. But there's a lot to be gained by fortifying vulnerable muscle groups such as quadriceps and hamstrings.

I do most of my working out in the five months between the last game of the year and spring training—which gives me staying power during the season. I work out on Nautilus machines and with free weights every other day for ninety minutes. I strengthen my calves, hamstring, thighs, and pay extra attention to my stomach muscles to protect my back—which has given me some trouble over the years.

To make it fun and aggressive, I play baseball in my mind to get my adrenaline going. In my favorite scenario, the score is tied in the bottom of the ninth inning. There's a man on third, one out, and I've got a plane to catch in thirty minutes. The plane gives me extra incentive to work hard, and the game is won when I've completed my repetitions to satisfaction.

Remember, every young body becomes an old body, and the better shape you keep your body in, the better your body's going to serve you when you start piling up the years.

A PROPER DIET AND NO DRUGS

When Jim Rice first called me the Chicken Man, he was kidding around, but diet in sports is no laughing matter. I can't say that you are what you eat, but food sure has an effect. Chicken, for instance, doesn't sit heavily in your stomach, and it gives you energy without weighing you down. Chicken is easy to digest, and you'll perform better for having eaten it.

Red meat or pork, however, sits heavily in your stomach and builds up cholesterol in your body, which can clog your arteries and make it harder for your heart to do its job. My advice is to eat a lot of vegetables and fish, and stay away from too many sweets.

Another *don't* for athletes is drugs. There's no more tragic a loss than when an athlete falls to drugs. We've seen it in basketball, football, baseball, and track. Drugs not only sabotage your concentration, they can also ruin your health and even end your life.

If you want to feel high, practice your hitting. Perfect your slightly-up swing. Learn to hit the opposite way. Lay down a sacrifice bunt. Work on your hit-and-run. Master the Power Curve and utilize the Impact Zone to your full potential. The fact is, there's no free ride to success or satisfaction: you have to work at it. So, don't just become a Conscious Hitter—become a Conscious Person. Do with drugs what you do with pitches outside the strike zone. Just say no.

MAKE SURE YOU GET YOUR LICKS

Hitting is nothing if not experimentation, and there's no better place to test theories, sharpen skills, and groom good habits than at batting practice. Dwight Evans discovered a stance that turned him from a .270 to a .290 hitter at the age of thirty-five.

Batting practice is also the best place to develop the discipline and repetition that makes good hitters. I use it to rehearse big-game situations. My favorite scenario is a runner on third with two outs in ninth inning of the seventh game of the World Series. The game is tied, and my team can win it with a hit. All I have to do is drive the ball through the infield, and it's over. So, I don't swing at bad

Batting practice is where you develop discipline and repetition at the plate. Put yourself in game situations and apply the rules of good hitting when you swing. The better you hit in practice, the more likely you are to hit well in games.

pitches. I respect my strike zone and make each swing count.

The approach gets me used to hitting in real pressure situations and makes my practice time much more valuable. Whenever you take batting practice, aim to make solid contact eight out of ten times. Bat control is your main goal. So, practice hitting to each field and always swing to hit as hard and as far as you can—even if you're hitting on the ground.

SUPERSTITION IS THE WAY

Everyone I know who plays organized sports is superstitious. In baseball, players have their favorite underwear or glove, a certain meal they eat before the game, a lucky number, or a secret phrase. Superstitions may not be logical or account for what happens on the field. They're routines and rituals for the soul and spirit. They're part of your mental preparation for a game, and they contribute to Conscious Hitting by enhancing your confidence at the plate.

I didn't plan on having superstitions. They just happened as I grew up. If I got four hits one day, I'd remember something I did a little differently and do it again the next day. I didn't always repeat my performance, but if the ritual worked I kept it up.

My first charm was the Hebrew word *chai,* which means "life." The word looks like a combination of 7 and 17—my favorite numbers—and I used to draw the sign in the dirt in high school for luck. I also have always stepped on the chalk lines when

I take the field and over them when coming off.

These days, I arrive at Fenway Park for 7:35 P.M. starts at exactly 3:15 P.M. I weigh in at 197 lbs. before I play. I take ground balls at 4:00. I get a drink of water at 4:17. At 5:17, I loosen up for batting practice. I hit for five minutes at 5:30. At 5:35 I run around the bases. Then I return to the clubhouse and change into my game uniform. At 6:40, I come out to throw to prepare for infield practice. From 6:50 to 7:17—there's that number again—I run three long wind sprints and two short ones. Then, I'm ready to play.

I wear the same shoes, shirt, and pants every day when I'm doing well. Nothing changes until it has to change. If I go a couple of games without hits, I'll change my shirt and shoes. The value of superstition is using it to develop winning habits. So, if I've got a ritual that's not producing results, I'll drop it and pick up something that's working.

My favorite superstition, of course, is chicken—and I'll stake my average on the fact that it works. It began in the minors when I started eating fowl three or four times a week in 1977. I'd like to tell you I had an inkling that it was going to help, but the truth is, red meat was beyond my budget. After a while, I noticed that chicken felt lighter in my gut. Then, in spring training 1982, I went five for six against the Cardinals fresh off a lemon-chicken lunch. That convinced me that chicken had a positive effect on my game, and I've been eating chicken before games ever since.

Boggs and Brisson take a break at home plate.

When April rolls around, only one thing really matters:

BASEBALL!

And you can cover all the bases, even between games, with Perigee Books on everything from baseball lore to official baseball rules to fantasy baseball!

THE GREATEST STORIES EVER TOLD ABOUT BASEBALL
by Kevin Nelson

Whether you're an avid fan or a friend of one, you're sure to enjoy this fresh, irreverent look at our national pastime. Focusing on the players ("Owners do not play the game; they only screw it up"), Nelson eschews statistics in favor of the funniest anecdotes and tall stories in baseball lore. Filled with hundreds of quips and quotes from the sport's most colorful personalities, this is one hit you won't want to miss!

PETE ROSE ON HITTING
How to Hit Better Than Anybody
by Pete Rose and Peter Golenbock

Learn how to bat from the greatest hitter of all time! Using dozens of photographs, baseball star Pete Rose explains in easy-to-follow prose the practical techniques and mental qualities that can make you a winner at the plate. A one-of-a-kind guide for Little Leaguers, high school and college athletes, and major leaguers alike.

BASEBALL RULES IN PICTURES
New and Updated Edition
by G. Jacobs and R. McCrory

Now you can resolve the trickiest baseball disputes whether you're at the ballpark or in your living room! Featuring over 175 captioned illustrations in four sections (batter, pitcher, runner, and umpire) and highlighting actual playing situations, *Baseball Rules in Pictures* includes the complete text of the 1984 Official Rules of Baseball and a foreword by legendary umpire Ron Luciano. This easy-to-use, easy-to-read guide is the "last word" reference for baseball coaches, players, and fans.

OFFICIAL LITTLE LEAGUE BASEBALL RULES IN PICTURES
Introduction by Dr. Creighton J. Hale, President, Little League Baseball

Incorporating more than 150 line drawings, the full text of Little League's Official Playing Rules, and all the latest rule changes, this straightforward guide is an indispensable handbook for the two million youngsters who play Little League baseball every year. Parents, coaches, managers, and umpires will find *Official Little League Baseball Rules in Pictures* an essential companion on the field or in the stands.

THE FANTASY BASEBALL ABSTRACT 1990
by Wayne Welch

Build a championship fantasy baseball team with the help of *USA Today* columnist and veteran owner in one of the largest fantasy leagues in the country. This complete sourcebook for baseball lovers and fantasy players provides all the basics for getting started, along with a team-by-team analysis including full 1989 year-end statistics and predictions for the 1990 season.

STRENGTH TRAINING FOR BASEBALL
by Jose Canseco and Dave McKay
illustrated with over 100 photographs

Strength training is one of the newest, most revolutionary developments in the conditioning of baseball players. A stronger, healthier, well-conditioned player has the best chance to improve his statistics. With clear, concise language, Canseco, the star of the Oakland Athletics, and McKay, the team's fitness coach, demonstrate step-by-step the exercises that can give any player the winning edge.

MOST VALUABLE BASEBALL CARDS
by Christopher Benjamin

Most Valuable Baseball Cards contains full-size reproductions of the 400 most sought-after baseball cards—with a total value of over $300,000! It is an indispensable source of information on these collectibles and includes the history of the card, its approximate value with an explanation of that value, and a brief biography of the player.

Ordering is easy and convenient. Just call 1-800-631-8571 or send your order to:

The Putnam Publishing Group
390 Murray Hill Parkway, Dept. B
East Rutherford, NJ 07073
Also available at your local bookstore or wherever paperbacks are sold.

			PRICE	
		SBN	U.S.	CANADA
_____	*The Greatest Stories Ever Told About Baseball*	399-51227	$ 8.95	11.75
_____	*Pete Rose on Hitting*	399-51164	7.95	10.50
_____	*Baseball Rules in Pictures*	399-51597	6.95	9.25
_____	*Official Little League Baseball® Rules in Pictures*	399-51531	6.95	9.25
_____	*The Fantasy Baseball Abstract 1990*	399-51593	9.95	12.95
_____	*Strength Training for Baseball*	399-51596	12.95	16.95
_____	*Most Valuable Baseball Cards*	399-51592	10.95	14.50

Subtotal $_____

*Postage & Handling $_____

Sales Tax $_____
(CA, NJ, NY, PA)

Total Amount Due $_____
Payable in U.S. Funds
(No cash orders accepted)

*Postage & Handling: $1.00 for 1 book, 25¢ for each additional book up to a maximum of $3.50.

Please send me the titles I've checked above. Enclosed is my:

☐ check   ☐ money order

Please charge my

☐ Visa   ☐ Master Card

Card #_____ Expiration date_____

Signature as on charge card_____

Name_____

Address_____

City_____ State_____ Zip_____

Please allow six weeks for delivery. Prices subject to change without notice.